# Intentional Changes

# Intentional Changes

## A Fresh Approach to Helping People Change

**Allen Tough**

**Follett Publishing Company**
Chicago, Illinois

Atlanta, Georgia • Dallas, Texas
Sacramento, California • Warrensburg, Missouri

*Designed by Karen A. Yops*

**Library of Congress Cataloging in Publication Data**

Tough, Allen M.
  Intentional changes.

  Includes bibliographical references and index.
  1. Adult education.   I. Title.
LC5219.T59        374            82–1392
ISBN 0-695-81665-8               AACR2


First Printing

# Contents

## Figures

## Tables

# Foreword

I don't know which is more interesting—this book or its author.

Allen Tough is a deceptive man, but not intentionally. On several occasions when I have alluded to him as an explorer and adventurer in ideas, this comment has caused surprise and doubt: he seems so quiet. Until people think about it, they do not guess how far he has traveled, how many ideas and fields of inquiry and therapies and religions he has searched. He seems so aloof, so untouched by all the ferment and conflict of ideas. But he has been there and has experienced most of the tumult in thinking and feeling, while his own life proceeds steadily because he has made the decisions that govern it and carried them out.

While no poet, Allen does have the knack that some explorers have of talking about what has happened simply enough so that the rest of us can understand. Thus, he and Cyril Houle were the first to produce a clear image of the self-directed learner. Allen's language about the concept of self-directed learning has been so simple that some observers say, "The emperor has no clothes," not realizing that the most profound ideas in education may not appear in sophisticated dress or spew out of a computer. The whole world of education has not yet caught up with that basic concept, that learning is a part of all of us, but the circular waves from this single idea are growing and extending.

Learning is a fundamental concept and is always involved in some kind of change. Some people fear change, and many people talk about changes as if all were inevitable, and always to be desired. Of course, they are not: people need to fight as fiercely against some changes as on behalf of others. There can be choices with changes.

These days it is customary to repeat that millions of people in developing countries have precious little choice, pressed down and molded as they are by a crippling cycle of poverty, unemployment, malnutrition, disease, illiteracy, and often of political tyranny. When social forces are so devastating, where is there room for intentional change? Even in North America, the individual seems so impotent in the face of problems like pollution, armed aggression, the rape of natural resources: it seems that these forces cause all important changes rather than the intention of an individual.

It is precisely at a time when such views are omnipresent and lead to such pessimism and inertia that Allen Tough has chosen to look at people choosing to change. The questions are large and foundational because, whether we like it or not, we are all involved.

What does he find? At first, we may be somewhat disappointed. There are no revelations or vaunted claims. He follows his data carefully and, therefore, reports changes in insight or behavior, one step at a time—not by great transforming leaps. But he is aware that children learn to balance and walk before they can run or vault or plunge or soar. Or travel in packs. The tidings are about the ordinary, daily activities of people like us when they determine to change and what supports or inhibits that decision. In the process, vague but unmistakable outlines of a picture are beginning to form, of some changes that may be possible, how they may be blocked or assisted, and the role of the chief actor: *the person who chooses to change.*

Allen Tough is an individual who, for twenty years, has been persistent in working a "mother lode," literally a priceless vein of information because it opens up some treasures for education, therapy, and political development. He has been a solitary figure, but has also worked well with colleagues and students (and all of his students soon become colleagues) and his work reflects their shared insights.

This book does not provide a complete picture or scenario. How could it? It lacks examination of the fascinating changes associated with the violence of revolutions. The changes reported, while significant, are not of the depth or profundity referred to in the phrase "paradigm shift." But that may come. Allen has found a question worth probing and a means of better understanding and reporting on human behavior. He has begun to explore in a different dimension than most psychologists or novelists what it means to change. He brings back news, and there will be more to come from fellow explorers.

J. Roby Kidd
Ontario Institute for Studies
in Education, Toronto

# Preface

This book focuses on the total array of intentional changes that people achieve in themselves and their lives. The early chapters describe the content and size and importance of these changes and then turn to the question of who chooses, plans, and implements them. This fresh picture of intentional changes is based on intensive interviews with 330 men and women. The rest of the book spells out various implications for professional practitioners, policymakers, and researchers. I have become convinced that we can all do much more to encourage and help intentional changes if we understand the person's natural process of change.

As far as I can discover, this is the first book to focus comprehensively and exclusively on the total range of intentional changes. A combination of manual and computer searches of *Psychological Abstracts, Sociological Abstracts, Social Science Index*, ERIC, and library card catalogs failed to turn up any similar book or paper.

This book fills a gap between two other sorts of books. On the one hand lie many psychology books dealing with maturation, psychological development through the life span, personality change, and learning. Most of these books dealing with human changes have fused together intentional and unintentional changes without distinguishing between the two. They examine various outcomes or changes in the person regardless of the extent to which the person was seeking or striving for those changes. Their focus is quite legitimate and appropriate for their purposes, but I believe professional practitioners, policymakers, and researchers can also benefit from focusing specifically on those changes that are intentional.

On the other hand lie books that deal exclusively with intentional changes, but only within one area of life or through one method. There are, for example, numerous books available on intentional changes within the areas of job, parenting, physical health, marriage relationships, sex, emotions, and spiritual growth. There are many books, too, on one intentional change method or path, such as counseling, psychotherapy, education, medicine, encounter groups, meditation, religion, journal writing, behavior modification, travel, buying a house, winning a fortune, hypnosis, bioenergetics, Gestalt, dream interpretation, and running. Such books are important and useful, but they do not provide a comprehensive picture of the person's natural process in the entire range of intentional changes. This book is intended to fill that gap.

*Intentional Changes* is written for professionals, policymakers, and the academic community in several fields concerned with intentional changes: counseling and personal growth, lifelong learning for adults, psychology, the self-help movement, the women's movement, secondary and higher education, health, social work, humanistic and transpersonal psychology, personal transformation, psychotherapy, and religion. The book will not only give such readers a better understanding of a central phenomenon in their fields, but will also suggest several specific implications for improved practice and policy and for future research. The early chapters of the book may also be useful for lay readers who want to understand their own changes better, but they were not written with this purpose in mind.

In much of my earlier work I studied the adult's major learning efforts and "learning projects" (Tough, 1967, 1979). The present book widens that focus to include the entire range of intentional changes, regardless of whether they were achieved by a series of intentional learning episodes or in some other way. These various ways of achieving an intentional change are discussed in the section on "How the Person Implements the Change" in chapter 4. This book both confirms (because the findings exhibit a similar pattern) and enlarges the research on the adult's learning projects. For example, it demonstrates that men and women are remarkably successful at choosing, planning, and implementing intentional changes, with most help being obtained from friends and family rather than from books or professionals.

My recent research did not focus on why people make changes, although much can be inferred from their choices. Penetrating insights into why adults choose to change will require much further study.

This book is based on interviews with 330 men and women. Of these 330 interviews, 180 were conducted during the process of developing the final interview schedule, or were conducted by graduate students as course projects. These 180 interviews contributed significantly to the ideas for this book, but their quantitative data have not been included.

The quantitative data have come from the other 150 interviews. In six of these interviews, however, no intentional change could be identified: these nonchangers are discussed in chapter 3. The 150 interviews were conducted face-to-face and took an average of one hour. They were conducted between 1977 and 1980 by current and recent graduate students in adult education who had received training in interviewing.

The 150 interviews took place in three locations in each of three countries. They were conducted in Canada (Toronto, semirural Ontario, and Nova Scotia), in the United States (Pittsburgh, rural Vermont, and Ames, Iowa), and in England (Worcestershire, Nottinghamshire, and Leicestershire). Because I had to rely mostly on interviewers whom I knew rather than on an international survey research organization, the particular locations were largely determined by the cities in which the interviewers lived. In general, though, the nine locations provide a good variety and are unlikely to be biased overwhelmingly in one particular direction. Given the resources for about 150 interviews, I opted for spreading them over several populations and geographical areas instead of selecting a sample of 150 from a single narrow population. Within each location the interviewers tried to sample the adult population, age 25 and over, with as little bias as possible. Most of the interviewees were selected at random from the municipal voters' or assessment lists or from the telephone book. Some were selected by knocking on doors in various neighborhoods. We excluded persons living in nursing homes and other institutions, and persons who could not speak English well enough to be interviewed.

The 150 interviewees came from various walks of life and from all age ranges between 25 and 85: 45% were between 25 and 39 years old, 43% were between 40 and 59, and 12% were 60 and over. Fifty-five percent were men, and 45% were women. The interviewers classified 28% as lower and working class, and 72% as middle and upper class. To record the highest educational qualification that the person had completed, we used the following categories (slightly adapted for the British interviews): less than grade 10 (19%), secondary school graduation (34%), one or two years of post-secondary education (18%), more advanced qualifications (29%). Data on race were collected only in the United States (73% were white) and in England (all were white).

Because of inevitable sampling errors and response errors, we cannot be certain whether similar results will be found in large-scale studies in other locations in the future. No doubt the numbers will change somewhat as future researchers survey other nations and other parts of the United States, the United Kingdom, and Canada. I am confident, however, that the general picture will prove to be reasonably accurate for many populations, even though the particular figures will vary a little. As the interview data arrived in my mail from a great diversity of interviewers in widely scattered regions, I was struck by the remarkable consistency in the basic patterns from one sample to another.

All of the interviewees mentioned so far were at least 25 years old. In addition, one section of chapter 2 describes the changes achieved by approximately 100 children and adolescents.

I want to express my gratitude for the important contributions that several persons have made to this book. Most of the interviews were conducted by Heibatollah Baghi, David Blackwell, Stephen Brookfield, Bill Brown, Joan Caesar, Judith Calder, Jeanne Eddington, Connie Leean, Elizabeth McCombs, Henry McGrattan, Judy O'Brien, Harvey Roach, Deborah Stewart, Marie Strong, and Marsha Young. I am also grateful to their interviewees, who were so willing to give their time and their personal story.

Larry Orton, Barry Walker, and Margaret Brillinger performed various tasks at a high level during their graduate assistantships. David Blackwell provided useful ideas and encouragement. Schmuel Hirschfeld, along with his friend DEC-10, performed much of the data analysis. Isabelle Gibb used her interlibrary loan skills to obtain many of the books cited in the text. Elaine Posluns, Barry Walker, Schmuel Hirschfeld, and Joan Neehall reacted thoughtfully to early drafts. Pat Anagnostakos provided excellent secretarial skills and typed the first draft. Julianna O'Brien cheerfully typed the second and third drafts. I am also grateful to various students and staff members at the Ontario Institute for Studies in Education for their insights and support over the years.

In Jean Lesher I have been fortunate to find the ideal executive editor: insightful, enthusiastic, quick, and helpful.

The family caring and encouragement that have been so important to me during my five years of work on this book were provided by Elaine, Susan, and Paul. I also want to mention my mother and father; their recent experiences have taught me much about unintentional and intentional changes.

# Chapter 1

# Focusing on Intentional Changes

Intentional changes are fascinating and important. Men and women bring about remarkable changes in themselves and their lives. They develop self-awareness, become physically fit, change a personal relationship, move to a new job, or grow spiritually. They increase their understanding of human nature, ecology, current events, or the universe. They change their home or lifestyle, begin a new recreational activity or volunteer activity, add a child to their family, or break a destructive habit or addiction.

To achieve these changes, people choose a wide variety of paths and methods along with a great diversity of helpers and books. Many persons are remarkably successful at achieving their chosen changes and proceed largely without professional help. Their own natural process of intentional change is highly effective, and they obtain help from friends and relatives. Some changes, however, do rely on help from a professional person, such as a counselor, teacher, group leader, doctor, therapist, religious leader, training and development specialist, or social worker.

Sometimes the decision to change requires a great deal of effort and time. Should I get married or shouldn't I? Should we have a third child? Will a new job really be better than my present one? Is the thrill of skydiving worth the costs and risks? Sometimes the steps to achieve the change require a great deal of effort or will-power. Breaking a habit, learning a complex skill, becoming a marathon runner, and understanding current political and economic affairs are examples. In some intentional changes, though, both the choice and the steps are quick and easy.

## A Precise Focus

This book focuses exclusively on highly intentional changes. Many other changes occur too, of course, but I have found it very useful to focus specifically on changes that are highly intentional. In such changes the person clearly chooses the particular change and then takes one or more steps to achieve it.

In interviews in several parts of the United States, Canada, and England, we asked women and men to tell us about their largest, most important intentional change during the past two years. We focused on the portion of the originally chosen change that had, in fact, been achieved: we wanted to study their largest actual change, not their largest intention!

We excluded changes that were desired or chosen but not achieved, such as an unsuccessful effort to switch jobs. We excluded a thoughtful decision to *not* change, such as a person's decision to continue in the present job after receiving an attractive job offer elsewhere.

During the early interviews I wrestled with the question of just how intentional the changes had to be in order to be included. In order to focus on the most useful phenomenon to understand and facilitate, I have adopted a tough stand on just how intentional the change must be. It has to be *highly* intentional, not just somewhat or fairly intentional. Let us turn now to the details of just how intentional a change must be in order to be included in our interviews and in this book.

To be considered sufficiently intentional, a change must have two major characteristics. First, the change must be definitely chosen and intended. That is, the person clearly makes a decision to change in a particular direction. Second, the person then takes one or more steps to achieve the change. The person does something specific, rather than passively letting the change occur with no effort at all. Choosing and striving are the two key elements: the person chooses a particular change and then takes action to achieve it. We exclude changes that do not involve both a clear choice and some specific efforts or steps. To make these two elements clearer in our interviews, they were displayed in a diagram (sheet #1 in the Appendix).

At the time it is chosen, the desired change may be fairly broad in the person's mind rather than perceived narrowly or in great detail. Such a change is sufficiently intentional if the broad area of change is definitely in the person's mind. For instance, a person may anticipate only the broad general type of change, not the detailed specific changes, when choosing a powerful path, such as psychotherapy, a spiritual quest, an insight-producing drug, or an assignment abroad.

For example, I once decided to travel alone to India to teach at the University of Rajasthan for two months. My decision was motivated by a fairly broad desire to learn about India in general: at that stage I did not have in mind any particular aspects that I wanted to learn about. Soon after I arrived, however, the impact of the poverty all around me was so great that I focused my learning efforts on certain particular aspects, such as the causes of poverty in less developed nations and the steps required for economic development. I count this as an intentional change because it clearly fits within my initial broad goal of learning about India.

The other major impact of my two months abroad was a sharp awareness of the importance to me of my family. I do not count this as intentional because I had not anticipated it nor chosen it. The decision to travel to India was intentional, of course, and I knew that such a powerful experience might produce unexpected sorts of changes. I count a change as intentional, however, only if the person expects and definitely seeks the approximate sort of change that does occur.

When I say that the person must choose the change, I am referring to a conscious choice and intention of which the person is clearly aware. I agree with the notion that, at a level below our awareness, we sometimes choose or intend an apparently accidental or chance event. Poor health, a miraculous cure, or being victimized, for example, may be "chosen" and sought by the person at a subconscious level. This phenomenon has been described by Schutz (1979) in his chapter on "Choice." Although I recognize the importance of these changes, I do not include them in this book.

Also, I include only changes that are primarily chosen *voluntarily*. That is, the "choice" is not largely forced on the person or virtually required by the circumstances. The person is not primarily coerced into making the change. It is not required in order to avoid some immediate consequence that the person perceives as a disaster, such as being fired, divorced, or killed. If a boss threatens to fire a secretary unless daily output increases, if a spouse threatens divorce unless the couple tries to conceive a child, if a person's salary is cut in half because of the employer's financial situation, then I would call the resulting changes forced and coerced, not voluntary and highly intentional.

Our focus also excludes intentional *responses* to an unintended event that reduces rather than increases the person's options. For instance, a man may be fired, his spouse may die, or he may develop a life-threatening illness. After this sudden unintended traumatic event occurs, the man may have some choice of how to react to that change. He may even choose a very courageous, unexpected, unusual, fresh course of action. He may obtain a job in another field, marry a quite different sort of woman, or become a marathon runner. I do not see these as highly intentional changes: each is simply an intentional *response* to an unintentional change. In each example, the man did not make the initial decision of whether to change: he merely chose one option from those remaining.

## Benefits from Focusing on Intentional Changes

It would be foolish for me to claim that only intentional changes are important. They are important, of course, but so are unplanned external events, deliberate influence from others, maturation, and changes at the subconscious level. For instance, I am highly aware of the powerful effects of newspapers, magazines, and TV on my views and values. Also, in the past few years I have become impressed by the powerful impact of my ongoing subconscious stream of events, feelings, dreams, and conflicts. I try to be aware of what is happening in this rushing underground stream, but can do little to control it. From reading and from a few personal experiences, I also recognize that there are certain situations in which it is sometimes valuable to let go, to cease all intending and striving; some examples are a trance state, a mystical or cosmic union experience, and certain moments in athletics.

All in all, then, I would never deny the power and significance of unintentional changes. At the same time, I do claim that professional helpers and researchers can gain important benefits from focusing specifically on intentional changes.

Many occupations and professional fields foster and facilitate intentional changes. Examples are management development, counseling, therapy, human growth groups, lifelong learning and adult education, professional development, career and life planning, humanistic psychology, secondary schools, higher education, health professionals, social work, rehabilitation, staff development, supervision, performance appraisal, behavioral self-management, libraries, religious and spiritual leaders, and transpersonal psychology. The entire range of intentional changes may provide a useful context within which to view your own particular helping efforts. Also, a better understanding of the person's natural ongoing process of intentional change will lead to greater effectiveness as a helper. Obviously, too, we can be far more helpful in the person's process of choosing and planning *intentional* changes than we can be with unintentional changes. People are unlikely to seek our help with their accidental changes, but may welcome better help with their voluntarily chosen changes.

Research and theory, too, could probably benefit from this fresh and comprehensive focus. The total range of intentional changes is an appropriate, useful, powerful focus for both research and theory-building. Our fundamental understanding of human behavior may be enhanced through studies of intentional changes. Such changes are at least as common and significant as unintentional changes, as chapter 3 will demonstrate.

In *The One Quest,* the widely known psychiatrist Claudio Naranjo has attempted to integrate the apparently diverse paths for change that people choose within education, psychotherapy, and religion. He stated that "if we examine closely the nature of the separate quests for growth, sanity, and enlightenment we may discover enough of a meeting ground among them to warrant the ambition of a unified science and art of human change" (1972, p. 30). Surely the appropriate time has arrived for many researchers to move ahead in developing a unified science of intentional human change.

Finally, you may have a personal as well as professional interest in intentional changes. They are fascinating to explore and are often discussed. For instance, successful and unsuccessful efforts to change one's job, relationships, habits, body, or home are common topics of conversation.

A second personal benefit arises because we often provide help to a friend, neighbor, or relative in addition to providing professional help to our students, clients, or patients. Each of us is, re-markably often, part of the social environment to which someone turns for help with an effort to change. By understanding the natural process of intentional changes, we may become even more thoughtful and effective as helpers.

A third personal benefit concerns our own changes. Each of us must decide quite often whether or what to change, and how to do so. We may choose and achieve our changes more effectively after we gain greater insight into intentional changes in general. My impression is that most of us, though already reasonably successful in managing our own changes, could become even more thoughtful and competent in this sphere.

# Chapter 2

# Areas of Change

Important intentional changes are particularly common in four areas: (1) job, career, and training; (2) human relationships, emotions, and self-perception; (3) enjoyable activities; and (4) residence location. These four areas account for 75% of all intentional changes.

This picture emerged from interviews with 150 American, British, and Canadian men and women. Details regarding the samples are given in the preface. These interviews used an intensive probing approach and leisurely dialogue to elicit the person's largest, most important intentional change during the preceding two years. The interviewer allowed plenty of time for the person to recall various intentional changes from the past two years and to choose the largest one. The questions, diagram, and probe sheet used to enhance recall are reproduced in the Appendix. With or without using those aids, you might benefit at this stage from recalling your own largest intentional change during the past two years.

David Blackwell and I worked at categorizing the particular changes into several areas or clusters. At first we worked quite independently. Each of us wrote the particular changes on slips of paper, and then moved these around on our respective dining room tables until some clusters emerged that were reasonably clear-cut. We then compared our lists, which turned out to be remarkably

25

similar, and moved toward a list containing nine areas of change.

Shorthand labels for the nine areas are given in table 1, and fuller descriptions are provided in this chapter and by Blackwell (1981). Table 1 shows the percentage of changes that falls into each area.

## Career, Job, and Training

One-third of our interviewees chose a change related to their job or career as their largest and most important change during the previous two years. Within this broad area of change, several clusters are evident. The most common job-related change of all was to move from one job to another. A 28-year-old flight instructor, hoping eventually to be a pilot for a major airline, obtained a job as a copilot. As often happens with a job change, he had to move to another state for this promotion. A man in his late thirties left his job with a public transit system to become an independent long-distance truck driver. The interviewer commented that "this man's passion for trucking was evident when I arrived on Sunday evening: instead of watching the season's biggest football game on TV

**Areas of Change**

| Area | Percentage |
| --- | --- |
| Career, job, and training | 33 |
| Human relationships, emotions, and self-perception | 21 |
| Enjoyable activities | 11 |
| Residence location | 10 |
| Maintenance of home and finances | 7 |
| Physical health | 7 |
| Volunteer helping activities | 3 |
| Religion | 3 |
| Basic competence (in reading, goal-setting, driving, etc.) | 3 |

Note: Each figure indicates the percentage of adults whose largest, most important intentional change in the past two years falls primarily within the given area. N=144.

**Table 1**

he was reading trucking magazines, and he'd traveled more than 1300 miles on the road during the previous 48 hours!" A woman became the successful owner-manager of an Oriental restaurant. She talked at length about her first crisis of losing the head cook and her trip to New York City (her first trip there) to search for another cook. "Everybody thought I was crazy, going alone and all." A lithographer moved to a smaller company with a more personal atmosphere where he felt more appreciated and had greater variety in his work. We also interviewed a few people who had moved into paid employment after a few years without paid employment, and a few who greatly increased or decreased the amount of time spent at the job.

Especially when jobs are scarce, it is common for a person to shift responsibilities or projects within the same position. Only the activities change, not the title and usually not the salary. One government employee in Vancouver, for instance, managed to hurdle all the red tape required for a major shift in his responsibilities.

A few interviewees who operated their own small businesses made significant changes within them. Some changed their product line or office location. One had his sons take over more and more responsibility for the operation of the business. An Ontario farmer changed to corn as his major crop because it seemed safer for the long-term future for himself and his sons. One person developed a new way of making musical instruments, and another wrote and marketed a series of books about antiques.

For several interviewees, the largest change was a major effort to become more competent at certain job responsibilities. One young woman enrolled in a two-year graduate program in social work as preparation for employment. A car mechanic, already competent at repairing medium and large cars, taught himself about small-car engines. Predicting that microcomputer technology would be increasingly important in his field during the next ten years, a man became expert in this area by taking courses.

## Human Relationships, Emotions, and Self-Perception

We saw in table 1 that 21% of all intentional changes were in the area of human relationships, emotions, and self-perception. We turn first to changes in particular relationships and then move on to more general changes.

Many persons reported changes in their closest existing human relationships. They changed how they were relating to a parent, spouse, or child. An 83-year-old man stopped handing over large sums of money whenever his 56-year-old son needed it. Other parents reduced their efforts to influence their children as the children reached their late teens, or changed their child-raising approach with younger children. Some men became more involved with their families and decreased their time at other activities. People improved their primary relationship through developing their acceptance of their own feelings, through changing their sexual behavior, through decreasing sex-role stereotypes, and so on. In a related study, a wide range of intentional changes to improve one's marriage relationship has been found by Margaret Brillinger in a doctoral dissertation in progress at the Ontario Institute for Studies in Education, University of Toronto. The most common changes in her study were communications (self-disclosure, listening, asking), attitudes and expectations toward self and partner, scheduling of time together, and entrance into counseling or a group learning experience.

Another kind of change involves adding someone to one's household or to a central place in one's life. People decide to have a particular person as best friend, for instance, or to begin a new primary relationship, or to live together or be married, or to have or adopt a child.

The opposite sort of change is to arrange for someone to leave one's household, or to greatly decrease a significant relationship. Separation and divorce are common examples. Because her 92-year-old father was becoming too great a drain while living with her, one interviewee arranged for him to move into a nursing home. She reported her benefits as "happier husband, happier me, relief, less stress, more time."

Rather than changing some particular relationship, many persons set out to change in more general ways within the area of human relationships, emotions, and self-perception. Some gained self-awareness and self-insight, and some gained greater self-esteem, self-confidence, or self-acceptance. People also reported becoming more assertive, more willing to follow their own interests and needs, more willing to speak out in groups and take the initiative, more liberated from attitudes and behavior that are sex-role stereotyped. In order to achieve changes in this general area, several interviewees chose a powerful ongoing method, such as individual psychotherapy or a Gestalt group.

Intentional changes in the area of human relationships, emotions, and self-perception have been particularly salient since 1965 or so.

Even 130 years ago, however, this area of change was recognized and discussed. For instance, in a book (Grey and Shirreff, 1851) outlining how women can change and learn and educate themselves, a section of more than six pages is devoted to developing self-insight and self-knowledge.

It is interesting that many of the changes in this area focused on one particular relationship, or one fairly specific goal or problem. In contrast, many psychotherapists and human growth groups focus on much more general and comprehensive sorts of changes, such as broad-gauge personality change. Strupp and others (1977, p. 96) have pointed out that "most mental health professionals tend to view an individual's functioning within the framework of some theory of personality structure": as a result, their views and diagnoses do not always fit with the individual's own assessment and with the opinion of society.

## Enjoyable Activities

Several interviewees told of adding, expanding, or modifying a specific enjoyable activity, or increasing their involvement in such an activity. These activities included social activities, a new circle of friends, sports, hobbies, crafts, art, theater, music, travel, hiking, cross-country skiing, sailing, traveling in a houseboat, and other recreational activities.

A prosperous 72-year-old farmer who had never before traveled outside the state of Vermont began taking vacation trips to major cities such as Washington and Quebec. On one of these trips he experienced his first flight on an airplane. On the trip to Washington, D.C., "I saw more than most people do who live right there. The traffic made me nervous, though, and the people and the fast pace. I was always worrying we'd get lost, but Mrs. said there was no reason to worry because we could always get a taxi to take us back to the hotel. I'm more interested in the news now—enjoy seeing famous buildings in the news from Washington."

Some major learning efforts fit better in one of the other areas of change, such as job or maintenance, but learning about something for interest or enjoyment fits best in the present area. A resident of an old British town, for instance, recently began spending a great deal of time studying local history and architecture because of fascination and enjoyment.

For two interviewees, the largest intentional change was cutting back on a particular enjoyable activity. A 75-year-old man reduced the amount of time spent at his hobby, which was the development of an extensive collection of wrenches bought at farm auctions. A 69-year-old man had been bowling and curling with the same group for 30 years. He quit that team so that he was free to play on different teams as he chose.

## Residence Location

A move from one home to another was the largest, most important change for 10% of the people we interviewed. One young woman moved from an apartment to her first house. Several moved from a bustling city to a rural area.

In addition to the new physical surroundings and neighborhood, a change in residence can also involve a change in one's living arrangements. One might be sharing space with new people, for example, or be living alone for the first time. One person moved from a house with relatives to a bachelor apartment, another from her own apartment to her daughter's home, and one woman moved into a nursing home that she chose herself.

Sometimes the main change is to live apart from someone. One woman moved in order to be away from her adult sons because they were often visited by her estranged husband.

Other interviewees moved from one home to another and yet did not select that as their largest change. Moving from one apartment to another nearby, for instance, can be a fairly small change. Moving to a new job can require moving to a new city as a subsidiary change.

## Maintenance of Home and Finances

Sometimes one's largest intentional change occurs within the area of maintaining a suitable home, car, and pattern of personal finances. Common examples are building a patio or making some other improvement to one's home, buying furniture or equipment for the home, and buying a car.

An American couple, for example, completely winterized their home during the past two years with new windows, insulation, and a new roof: the house was a 100-year-old horse barn that the couple are gradually turning into a lovely rustic home. A British couple spent 18 months in a trailer on a rural plot of land they had bought. The land contained a derelict cottage. They renovated this cottage enough to move into it in December, even though the cottage did not yet have water or electricity. One man selected his newly acquired skill in woodworking as his most important change.

These days most of us can identify with the 44-year-old home-maker in Iowa whose change was "living more economically and making better choices in purchasing." She achieved this change through listening to consumer programs on television and radio, and through reading. Through the support of a peer self-help group for people who had become deeply in debt, one man threw away his credit cards and shifted to using only cash. He knew he had succeeded when he made it through the next Christmas season with absolutely no debts.

## Physical Health

Many intentional changes in the area of physical health are dramatic or at least clearly discernible. Several interviewees quit smoking, one stopped drinking with the help of an Alcoholics Anonymous group, and several became physically fit (and often simultaneously lost weight) through an exercise program. A woman with arthritis of the spine changed from her long-standing doctor to one with a different treatment approach.

The diversity of factors leading to a decision to change is well illustrated by one of the people who quit smoking. He had smoked for sixteen years and had finally quit two years before the interview. Here are some of the events and factors that he mentioned as leading up to his decision: "I read about the danger of lung cancer though I did not search specifically for this sort of reading material; I saw a TV program on lung cancer; my wife pointed out that I had started coughing; when I went out in the cold, I, too, noticed that my coughing was a problem; smoking is a dirty habit and produces nicotine fingers; it makes me fidgety and agitated; smoking contributes to my poor self-image."

A British woman's health change was seen by the interviewer as part of a broader reorientation. The specific change was to "a wholefood diet" that emphasizes organically grown vegetables, free-range farm products, and unprocessed food. The interviewer described this woman as vigorous, energetic, well-liked, approachable, personable, and able to cheerfully complete a range of commitments. His view is that "the specified intentional change could be regarded as the most visible index of a broader cultural reorientation: making the personal commitment to a wholefood diet reflected a wider involvement in ecological matters and volunteer activity with the local wholefoods-ecological group as a valuable publicist and fundraiser." That involvement led, in turn, to her becoming a candidate in the local council election as the representative of a newly formed conservation-conscious party. She also took courses in politics, sociology, local history, and ecology.

## Volunteer Helping Activities

Sometimes one's major change occurs in volunteer activities to help other people, in volunteer activities to improve the local community or the world, or in very large charitable donations.

For instance, a self-employed 46-year-old woman "became more giving of time, energy, and understanding. I try to spend 60% of my time giving out. I consciously make two phone calls or visits every week to an elderly or sick person, baby-sit, and generally try to be supportive to people." A 72-year-old retired editor went with her sister-in-law to a Catholic charismatic movement service, and then "I began trying to model myself after the other members, who show great depth of charity to others." She now does some errands for the senior citizens near her home and drives one woman to stores and appointments. In Nova Scotia, a dentist donated his time to set up a volunteer dental clinic in an old-age home. A 47-year-old professor in Vancouver sponsored a Vietnamese refugee who now lives with him. A 76-year-old woman developed and published a game based on her extensive study of the Bible.

## Religion

Some people achieve major changes in their religious practices or spiritual insights. A 65-year-old janitor in Iowa gained spiritual and religious understanding by reading and by attending study groups. A 27-year-old man in Newfoundland changed from having little interest in religion as an inactive Protestant to being an active Roman Catholic. A 46-year-old homemaker in Nova Scotia changed her relationship with God. She intentionally set out to achieve inner happiness through a better and clearer understanding of God and religion. An Ontario man began to set aside time each day for religious devotions, beginning with a 31-day published schedule received in the mail. An earlier study by Wickett (1977) found that a great many activities, such as cross-country skiing or liturgical dance, can be deliberate paths toward greater closeness to God.

To understand basic reality or to grasp the ultimate meaning of life, some people choose a somewhat different focus that is remarkably close to being spiritual or religious. For example, some try to gain perspective or wisdom through a broad understanding of history, the social sciences, or the long-term future of life in the universe. Some struggle to choose and then answer the basic or ultimate questions in life. Some describe their quest as a search for a philosophy of life, for an understanding of the meaning and purpose of life, for consciousness expansion, for mystical experiences or cosmic union, for an encounter with ultimate reality or the fundamental nature of the universe. The methods for all these goals cover a wide spectrum: meditation, private prayer, reflection, reading, writing, discussion groups, wilderness solitude, sexual union, music, astral travel, training in extrasensory perception, psychedelic chemicals, the deep symbolic and mythical levels described by Grof (1975), high dreams, and simply letting go. This paragraph is based on early exploratory interviews and on conversations over the years with various people; none of the changes in our 150 final interviews fits this paragraph.

## Basic Competence

Sometimes a person sets out to improve some basic competence or skill. In this area I am thinking of a broad or basic competence, potentially applicable in more than one area of life. Job competence, interpersonal skill, or a specific recreational skill would fit into other categories in table 1.

Here are some examples from the various interviews:

1. reading effectively at faster speeds,
2. driving a car,
3. thinking creatively and using problem-solving skills,
4. becoming more open-minded and inquiring, seeking an accurate picture of reality,
5. becoming competent in self-directed learning,
6. setting goals and priorities, and managing time effectively,
7. getting a general liberal education in order to be broadly knowledgeable and competent (not primarily for enjoyment or for a particular career),
8. gaining an extensive knowledge of current events and social conditions around the world.

## Some Reflections on the Changes

As I reflect on the intentional changes found by various interviewers, several thoughts come to my mind.

Before any of the interviews, I tried to predict the sorts of changes they would uncover. Looking back now at my early list, I realize that everything in it was a single, neat, clearly defined event such as having a baby, switching to another job, or moving. In fact, many changes turn out to be not so clear-cut. Some changes are largely internal (psychological or spiritual) rather than external. Several changes involve two levels: (1) several particular changes, and (2) a broad, underlying direction or theme, such as being more independent, more assertive, more willing to use power, more direct in communicating feelings, more spontaneous.

In a supplementary analysis, I categorized changes as primarily occurring in the external world, in the person's activities, or in the person's inner and outer behavior. About 16% of all intentional changes were primarily changes in the person's environment. Examples are residence location, adding a significant person to one's household, buying or selling something, and remodeling one's home. About 42% are changes in one's activities, in how one spends one's time. Examples are a new job, changed responsibilities within the same job, new recreational activities, and volunteer activities to help others. The other 42% are primarily changes in the person himself or herself. Examples: becoming physically fit, gaining basic understanding or perspective, modifying one's habitual behavior (stop smoking or stop losing one's temper).

One sort of change I did not anticipate at all is developing some new product or invention. For instance, one person patented a new musical instrument (a job change), and another person developed and published a 52-card Bible verse game (as a volunteer helping activity). My own largest change during the past two years has been to devote a major portion of my time to working on this book.

I have become increasingly certain that intentional change is often a natural and healthy component in a person's life. It is wrong to assume it is a sign of severe difficulty, illness, or a highly unsatisfactory life. It is more appropriate to empathically grasp and treasure another person's changes than it is to judge or criticize them. It is rarely correct to consider one area or type of change as inherently better than all others, or inherently worse or more dangerous or unimportant.

Many changes could be intended in either direction. For example, some interviewees increased the amount of time spent at work and some reduced it. One mother stopped "sitting on my tongue" with her children, and another stopped speaking up about her daughter's decisions. Other intended changes would almost always be in one direction, not the opposite direction. It is hard to imagine someone setting out deliberately to become less self-confident, for example, or less physically fit, less knowledgeable about the world, or less skilled at something.

When they first hear of my research into intentional changes, many people assume I am focusing on the adult life cycle. Although I have studied and taught the psychology of adult development, that is not the focus of this book. In fact, most of the changes in the interviews are not particularly related to the person's age or stage in life. When I first read each change (which was recorded at the top of the data sheet shown in the Appendix), I usually could not guess the person's age (which was at the bottom of the sheet).

Every change area in table 1 is the target of at least one major movement or enterprise. Programs in adult education, continuing education, lifelong learning, and the human growth movement try to facilitate change within several of the areas. Traditional counseling and psychotherapy touch on most areas at times. Self-help books are available to facilitate changes in almost every area. Peer self-help groups are springing up rapidly in several areas. No area seems particularly neglected or overlooked.

Almost all the changes reported to us are socially acceptable, or at least not widely condemned. Probably a few interviewees concealed an even larger change that they considered socially unacceptable. I find it hard to believe that, over a period of two years, not one of the 150 interviewees began a clandestine love affair that was a larger intentional change than the one reported to us.

## Variations in the Basic Pattern

The basic pattern for the areas of change was presented in table 1. We turn now to the patterns for various particular groups, shown in table 2.

Simply by looking at table 2, we can see that the basic pattern is remarkably consistent from one group to another. Job, career, and training is the most common area of change in every group except people in their sixties and older. Human relationships, emotions, and self-perception is the second most common area for almost all groups. Changes in enjoyable activities and residence location are fairly common in most groups. It is clear, then, that the relative

## Areas of Change in Several Groups

| | Job and Training | Relationships, etc. | Enjoyable Activities | Residence Location | Maintenance | Physical Health | Volunteer Activities | Religion | Basic Competence |
|---|---|---|---|---|---|---|---|---|---|
| **Country** | | | | | | | | | |
| Canada | 32 | 21 | 11 | 8 | 9 | 6 | 7 | 3 | 2 |
| England | 37 | 19 | 12 | 12 | 0 | 12 | 0 | 0 | 6 |
| USA | 38 | 21 | 10 | 14 | 7 | 3 | 3 | 3 | 0 |
| **Sex** | | | | | | | | | |
| Male | 38 | 17 | 13 | 6 | 10 | 5 | 5 | 4 | 1 |
| Female | 29 | 26 | 9 | 14 | 5 | 8 | 6 | 2 | 3 |
| **Age** | | | | | | | | | |
| 25-39 years | 43 | 28 | 11 | 8 | 3 | 3 | 2 | 2 | 2 |
| 40-59 years | 29 | 15 | 10 | 8 | 13 | 10 | 8 | 3 | 3 |
| 60 years and older | 12 | 18 | 18 | 24 | 6 | 6 | 12 | 6 | 0 |
| **Educational Level** | | | | | | | | | |
| Less than Grade 10 | 44 | 4 | 12 | 4 | 20 | 12 | 0 | 4 | 0 |
| Medium Education | 29 | 14 | 16 | 16 | 6 | 10 | 4 | 2 | 2 |
| Some Post-Secondary | 34 | 32 | 7 | 7 | 3 | 1 | 9 | 3 | 3 |
| **Social Class** | | | | | | | | | |
| Lower and Working Class | 37 | 17 | 10 | 10 | 12 | 10 | 0 | 2 | 0 |
| Middle and Upper Class | 32 | 22 | 12 | 10 | 6 | 5 | 8 | 3 | 3 |

Note: N=144. Each number is the percentage of interviewees in that group who reported the given area of change. For example, 32% of all the interviewees in Canada reported a job change. People in the medium education group ranged from those who had completed grade 10 through those who had graduated from secondary school or high school. People who had completed at least one year of post-secondary education were placed in the post-secondary group. For convenience in reading, the three levels of post-secondary education used in the statistical analyses have been combined here into a single category, and the four social classes have been reduced to two. Because of the small number of nonwhites, figures are not presented here for race.

**Table 2**

frequency of the various areas is remarkably consistent from one group to another. Although there certainly are differences among the groups, they do not overshadow the basic pattern.

We used a chi square test to see whether the distribution over the nine areas of change varied significantly (at the .05 level) from one group to another. No significant relationships were found between the areas of change and country, sex, age, or race. The areas of change did vary significantly, however, with educational level and with social class. When differences in sex were controlled for, it became apparent that the variation with educational level occurred largely among the men.

## Children and Adolescents

So far in this chapter, all of the interviewees have been at least 25 years old. Let's change our focus for a moment and look at teenagers and even younger children.

Informal conversations with children and adolescents have convinced me that they, too, make intentional changes. Here are some of the intentional changes that children age 15 and under have reported to me informally:

1. chose a best friend or a new dating partner,
2. chose a new circle of friends,
3. changed behavior with friends (for example, deeper genuine communication),
4. changed relationship and behavior with a parent,
5. became well informed on a subject through extensive reading in that area,
6. became skilled and knowledgeable with computers (through experimentation and friends),
7. discovered and followed own interests and preferences despite peer pressure,
8. chose a different enjoyable activity (new sport, hobby, craft, or recreational activity),
9. gained perspective on other cultures through travel,
10. improved fitness and health practices,
11. successfully sought self-understanding,
12. altered appearance (contact lenses, style and length of hair, clothing style),
13. chose a school,
14. chose and achieved a high level of academic performance,

15. chose a broad career path and particular school courses,
16. became more assertive in standing up for personal rights and
    wants.

An unpublished study by Fr. Harvey Roach focused specifically
on intentional change among children. He spontaneously adapted
our interview schedule to the language and concepts of each age
group. In Stoney Creek and Hamilton, Ontario, he interviewed ten
children at each age from 5 to 13, giving a total of ninety children.
The data from these children have not been included in any of the
data presented earlier in this chapter.

In his correspondence with me, Roach commented on the enthusiasm and animation with which the children described their intentional changes once they realized he was interested in freely chosen
changes, not changes required by school or home. "An example
was the thrill described by a 6-year-old when, after numerous at-
tempts, a strategy to ride a two-wheel bicycle gave her new mobil-
ity." Roach was struck by the ability of children to choose and
achieve changes, and he concluded that adults ignore or at least
underestimate this capacity in children. Certainly, very few adults
do much to foster and facilitate it.

In general, the changes of the older children were more varied,
more complex, more thoughtfully planned, and more self-directed
than those of the younger children.

Money and parental influence played important parts in affecting
some changes. "A 10-year-old girl no longer wishes to study the
organ after a year of instruction. Her parents invested $6 a week in
lessons and $3,500 in an organ. The lessons are continuing." An-
other example was provided by one of the persons for whom collecting a particular type of object was a major change: "One 7-year-
old was experiencing discouragement because the beer bottles he
was collecting were persistently cashed in by his father."

Almost all of the changes were in such enjoyable activities as
sports, games, hobbies, dance, music, arts and crafts, riding a bicycle, gymnastics, building models, and collecting. The changes of
only six children did not fit into that category. Five of them were 12
or 13 years old, and their five changes were as follows: sewing,
carpentry, study of encyclopedia, air cadets, religion. The other
child, age 7, had also changed in the religious area. I cannot explain
why several of the changes that arose in my informal conversations
with children did not arise in the Roach interviews.

# Chapter 3

# The Size and Importance of Intentional Changes

*The Benefits and importance of specific changes*

Many women and men succeed in producing significant changes in their environments, activities, and inner selves. They find these changes very beneficial to themselves and to others. While it is true that people resist certain changes, they definitely seek and achieve certain other changes.

This picture emerged clearly from our 150 interviews with men and women in various parts of the United States, Canada, and England. These interviews focused exclusively on intentional changes: the person chose the change and then took definite steps to achieve it. Specifically, the interviewer helped the person recall the largest, most important change during the two years before the interview.

This chapter presents our findings concerning the size and importance of the changes and the amount of benefit to the person and to others. One section then examines the phenomenon of non-change, and the final section examines unintentional changes.

## Size of Changes

It would be very difficult, time-consuming, and expensive to rigorously and objectively measure the size of each person's intentional change. This task would require a unique pretest and posttest for each particular change.

As an alternative, it is reasonably effective to simply ask the person how large and important the change was. Most people can estimate the size of their changes fairly accurately. From a list of four possible statements, we asked people to select the one that came closest to describing the size and importance of their intentional change. Here are the results:

- 31% chose the statement "a huge or enormous change, or of central importance in my life,"
- 40% chose "a fairly large and important change,"
- 26% chose "a definite change with *some* relevance and importance in my life,"
- 3% chose "small, trivial, petty, unimportant."

Most persons, then, do achieve quite a large significant change over a period of two years, according to their own assessment. Only 3% of the changes were reported as small, trivial, petty, or unimportant. Over 70% of the changes were at least fairly large and important.

At the beginning of the interview, some people were quite self-deprecating about the size of their changes, but then usually they felt much more positive after recalling and reflecting in detail. An earlier study found a similar phenomenon (Tough, 1967, p. 40). Apparently people have a negative stereotype about their capacity to choose and produce significant changes in themselves and in their lives. After an hour or more spent examining one of their actual changes, they become much more positive about their thoughtfulness and success in changing. People are generally much more capable of intentionally changing than the widespread stereotype indicates.

## Percentage of Goal Achieved

As another measure of how successfully people achieve their desired changes, we asked people to compare their originally chosen change and their actually achieved change. We asked, "What percentage of your desired change did you actually achieve?" Exactly half of the interviewees had achieved 100% of their desired change, but a few had achieved much less. The average (mean) amount achieved was 80%. Some persons changed even more than originally anticipated, but we studied only the portion that had definitely been chosen.

## Extent Noticed by Others

Here is another question we asked: "Now let's imagine a certain situation for a moment. Let's imagine that you describe your change to all your friends, relatives, neighbors, people at work, and everyone else who knows you. And then you say to each of these people, 'Have you noticed this change?' Approximately how many would say yes?"

The typical (median) answer was seven persons. Many (41%) of the interviewees said more than ten persons.

This question asked for very specific data, and is probably less likely to be influenced by inaccurate self-reporting or cognitive dissonance than broader questions are. The responses to this question support the other findings that the changes are large, significant, and noticeable.

## Amount of Benefit to Self and Others

To what extent do people benefit from their changes? Do changes lead to unhappiness, or to satisfaction and productivity? In an attempt to answer these commonly discussed questions with actual data, we asked people to tell us, "How much has this change contributed to your happiness, your satisfaction with life, or your well-being?" Here are the results (rounded off):

- 17% said "an enormous amount,"
- 34% said "a large amount,"
- 43% said "some definite benefit,"
- 4% said "little or nothing,"
- 3% said "it has done me more harm than good."

Clearly, intentional changes are usually seen as beneficial, and the person feels pleased rather than unhappy with their personal consequences.

The fear that personal changes are often harmful is certainly not confirmed by the data. Only 3% found that the change did more harm than good. One of these persons has such a simple but poignant story that I often think of it. Age 73 at the time of the interview, she had been employed and reasonably happy until her sons, who lived in a large city, persuaded her to give up her job and move to their city so she would be closer to them. "So I gave up my job, uprooted myself, and moved closer to my sons. Now I find my entire lifestyle has been altered. This change has not been a happy experience for me. My sons influenced me to make this change, but in fact I seldom see them."

Let us now turn to the amount of benefit for other persons. This topic brings us to a common misconception regarding intentional changes. Among my graduate students, among my friends, and in audiences to which I speak, I find a remarkable number of people who believe that such changes, especially if they are chosen and planned without professional help, are highly selfish. They equate "self-initiated and self-guided" with "selfish." Some people believe such changes are self-indulgent and use up energy and time that should be devoted to contributing to family, community, or society. Some people even go further and tell their favorite horror story about someone whose changes caused great pain to family and friends. A few believe that the community and nation would be better off, and people would be happier, if people reduced their changes.

Most changes are selfish in the sense that the person does benefit from them, as we have seen in the responses about whether the change contributed to "your happiness, your satisfaction with life, or your well-being." No doubt, too, one can find examples of changes that are unduly selfish and that hurt other people.

Most changes are of benefit not only to the person, however, but also to others. If we categorized all intentional changes as purely selfish, mixed, or purely a benefit to others, we would find very few examples in the two extreme categories. Individual change and social change are intertwined and interdependent, not separate and competing.

Here is the way we worded our question in the interview: "Let's set aside your own benefits for a moment, and look at any benefits for *other* people. Your change might already have been of some benefit to your family, your friends and relatives, your boss, other people in your organization, colleagues in your field, and so on. To what extent has your change provided some benefit to people other than yourself?" Here are the responses:

- 25% said "only to a small extent,"
- 36% said "medium amount; of some definite benefit to at least one or two persons,"
- 39% said "to a fairly large extent."

Obviously, intentional changes are not nearly as selfish as some critics suggest when they dismiss all personal change efforts as useless navel-gazing or irrelevant for society.

Some intentional changes do, of course, have adverse effects on other people, although Blackwell (1981) found that these effects were inconvenient or incommodious rather than harmful. For example, a few of his interviewees reported less time for family activities or home repairs. Two men were concerned about the effects that moving would have on their families, and one man inconvenienced his employer by quitting his job.

## Variations in the General Picture

We have now seen the general picture for five variables: size of the change, percentage achieved, extent to which the change was noticed by others, amount of benefit to self, and amount of benefit to others. Does this general picture vary significantly (at the .05 level) with age, educational level, social class, sex, country, race, or area of change? To answer this question we used a multiple analysis of variance for percentage achieved and a chi square test for all other variables, with an additional analysis for area of change using one-way analysis of variance. Of the 35 possible relationships, only 7 were statistically significant. Each of these will now be described.

The size of the change varied significantly with age, country, and area of change. The younger age group tended to have larger changes. The Americans tended to have larger changes with the Britons close behind, compared to the Canadians. Changes in residence location and in relationships were especially large, and the Sheffe procedure found that both of these groups (areas of change) were significantly different from enjoyable activities. Changes in volunteer activities and in religion were also comparatively small.

The percentage achieved did not vary significantly with any of the seven variables.

The extent to which the change was noticed by other people varied significantly with educational level. About 70% of the people in each educational level below a graduate degree reported that at least six persons noticed their change, whereas only 30% of those with a graduate degree reported this. The relationship between the extent noticed and the area of change was barely significant. Changes in residence location and physical health tended to be noticed by a relatively high number of persons, whereas changes in the areas of religion, basic competence, and volunteer activities tended to be noticed by relatively few.

The amount of benefit to the person's own happiness, satisfaction with life, and well-being varied significantly with age. People under 40 tended to report large or enormous benefits from their change, people between 40 and 59 tended to report a medium amount of benefit ("some definite benefit"), and people over 59 avoided the medium category and saw their benefits as either high or low.

The amount of benefit to other people varied significantly with nation. The Canadian groups tended to report higher benefits than the other two countries, and the people in England tended to be low.

In this chapter we have been discussing five measures of the size, importance, and benefits of intentional changes. To what extent are these five variables related to one another? The Pearson correlation coefficients are shown in table 3. As expected, all of these are positive. I would not have guessed, though, that the highest correlation would be between percentage achieved and extent noticed by others. The relatively high correlations between size and benefits are much easier to understand. It is interesting to see a reasonably high positive correlation between benefits to self and benefits to others, not a negative correlation as some critics of personal change might have predicted.

Only three correlation coefficients are not significant, and all three of them involve percentage achieved. I am surprised by this, and puzzled. I expected percentage achieved to show a high positive correlation with the other four variables.

## Nonchangers

Approximately 4% of the people with whom we began an interview were unable to identify any intentional change at all from the previous two years. As a 61-year-old woman put it, "I've changed absolutely nothing during the past two years, not even my brand of soap or my style of clothes." Because I am fascinated by nonchangers, I discussed these individuals at length with the interviewers.

Although none of the nonchangers could be described as joyful or outstandingly happy, they seemed reasonably contented and satisfied. As far as we could tell, they were quite genuine when they said they did not have much conscious desire to change themselves or their lives at the present time. One person seemed to speak for the group when he said, "Things are going OK, and I'm very comfortable, so I'm not motivated to do something new." Their emotional tone was generally even or flat, rather than marked by peaks

**Correlation Coefficients for Five Measures of Size and Benefits**

|  | Size | Percentage Achieved | Noticed by Others | Benefit to Self | Benefit to Others |
|---|---|---|---|---|---|
| Size |  | .06 | .14* | .29* | .22* |
| Percentage achieved | .06 |  | .34* | .10 | .06 |
| Noticed by others | .14* | .34* |  | .14* | .18* |
| Benefit to self | .29* | .10 | .14* |  | .20* |
| Benefit to others | .22* | .06 | .18* | .20* |  |

*Significant at the .05 level.

**Table 3**

and valleys. They were choosing a fairly safe path through life, rather than a path marked by adventure and change.

The nonchangers were generally *not* poor, illiterate, stupid, deprived, poorly educated, "disadvantaged," members of denigrated "minority" groups, nor living in adverse circumstances. In fact, some were upper-middle class, with above-average education. All of them had plenty of opportunities for intentional changes. These findings provide a sharp contrast to the picture of nonchangers held by some people.

Most nonchangers were busy with job, farm chores, child-raising, golf, friends, or whatever. Nonchange cannot be equated with low energy or little activity. In fact, some of their lives did contain minor unintentional changes that were caused by the environment or chosen by the spouse.

No doubt there are times for each of us when we fail to make a change that in fact would have been very beneficial for us. We sometimes let a bad situation go too long, for instance, without trying to change things. Although these situations do exist for all of us occasionally, and presumably for some people more often than for others, they are not nearly as common as I thought. My clear impression from the interviews is that the nonchangers are not really hurting themselves by choosing not to change. We asked all the interviewees to look back over the past two years and tell us about any change that they wanted but had not achieved. Most of their responses were mild and mundane and indicated that very few people are suffering much from their failure to seek or achieve certain changes.

My former reactions, the reactions of many students in my graduate courses on intentional change, and the reactions of some interviewers do not fit very well with reality. We are upset by nonchangers and assume there is something wrong with them. We assume they would be happier if they made certain changes. We wish everyone would change as much as we do. When talking about the nonchangers (or about our employees or spouse, perhaps!) we use the phrase "resistant to change." I now see that most of these reactions are inappropriate. Because some of us are deeply involved in choosing and guiding our own changes, we are threatened by people who are not. When we talk about resistance to change, we probably mean the person will not choose the particular changes or paths that we think best.

I end up convinced that change is not somehow better or more important than nonchange. On the contrary, the 80% or 95% of the person's characteristics and life that remains stable is probably at least as important as the portion that changes. Certainly people who accept the stable portion of their own qualities and lives, and who live effectively within the given situation, will typically be much happier than people who think only of change and of the future.

Changing too much can be at least as harmful to oneself as not changing at all. It can take time and emotional energy away from other activities that would provide greater happiness, or from family and job. It can lead to such preoccupation with change that people forget about all the beneficial nonchanging aspects of themselves and their lives. My impression of a few people is that they are constantly changing in order to avoid facing their loneliness, their emptiness, or some of their unpleasant characteristics. Changing too much during a year can greatly increase the chances of a serious illness (Holmes and Rahe, 1967).

Sometimes it is wise to choose nonchange. In the poignant ending of *Journey to Ixtlan* (1972), anthropologist Carlos Castaneda is clear on the next appropriate step in his pursuit of knowledge and change, but he decides to literally turn his back on that step and to leave the scene.

The best poem I have seen on the need of choosing nonchange at times was written by Dr. Robert MacIntyre in 1975. It is particularly meaningful to me because I was sitting beside him in a group meeting in my apartment when he wrote it, and because at that time I, too, was implementing too many major changes simultaneously. (I still refer to 1975 as "my year of changes.") Here are some lines from the poem, used with MacIntyre's permission:

Down, dawn, doom—out of the flow.
    Stop, stopping, stopped
        Stop expecting more!
        . . . . . . . . . . . . . . . . .
Mortal man of clay, heavy with unfired dross,
    only slightly warmed by flame of life.
        Striving, striving, starving
            to be more, less, different.
                Grow in awareness.
                Shrink in ego.
        Stupid, leaden, sullen, swollen striving.
            Why these endless goals, tasks, aspirations?
            There is no end.
            There is always another.
                Stop. Stop. Stop.
        . . . . . . . . . . . . . . . .
Come, live in the smaller world. Leave the flames of bliss
    to those who feel them. You will only consume yourself in them,
        implode into your own cold core.
        Stop wanting
            Stop trying
                Stop haunting
                    Stop vying
                        Stop stopping
                          Stop.

All of my thoughts so far in this section apply with certainty only to three countries: Canada, the United Kingdom, and the United States. They probably apply to certain other countries as well. In several other parts of the world, however, I have been deeply moved by the plight of people who have virtually no opportunities for beneficial change. They are nonchangers because of hunger, unending hard labor, overwhelming norms, and enormous restrictions, not because of their own free choice in the face of several good options. Such circumstances can exist in prisons, nursing homes, and elsewhere in the three countries in which we interviewed, but we did not sample these groups.

## Unintentional Changes

It is interesting to consider what proportion of major changes are intentional and what proportion are unintentional. In intentional changes, as chapter 1 pointed out, the person definitely and voluntarily chooses the change and then strives to achieve it by taking certain steps. I use the term *unintentional changes* to refer to all other changes, such as those caused by chance external events, maturation, subconscious influences, and so on. I have come across many people, including several of our interviewees, who believe that almost all human change is largely beyond the person's choice and control; it just happens. Toward the end of many interviews I have seen this stereotype shattered as people recall more and more of their active, deliberate, well-planned, successful efforts to bring about major change.

During our earlier interviews, the idea of asking about unintentional as well as intentional changes did not occur to me. Not until the last 56 interviews did we add such a question. During those 56 interviews, after the person had finished answering our questions about his or her largest, most important intentional change during the previous two years, we said, "We've been talking about a change that was chosen and intentional. Can you think of any unintentional change over the past two years—in yourself or your life— that is even larger and more significant than the change we've been discussing?" Just over half (55%) said no and the rest said yes. Their major unintended changes included separation and divorce, having a nervous breakdown, being fired, spouse being fired, improvement in the family business, unplanned pregnancy, having twins instead of one child, miscarriages, child's death, spouse's death, inflation, car needing to be replaced, and "finding a new girl friend." A 40-year-old engineer said, "Yes, smoking grass for the first time. This was unplanned, but it resulted in tremendous changes in my life."

Several other studies, too, suggest that approximately 55% to 70% of major changes during adulthood are intentional rather than unintentional.

Studying major personal changes in a group of Canadians working abroad, Filson (1975) found that the influence of the conscious process of considering and choosing the changes was slightly more important than the total impact of external forces and unconscious processes. He also found that 58% of all changes involved some time (usually more than 20 hours) at actively considering and weighing the change. That percentage was higher for men than for women, perhaps because "some of the married women preferred to let their husbands do their thinking for them with respect to the changes they were undergoing" (p. 66). The percentage was relatively high for occupational changes, relatively low for changes in personal awareness and feelings.

Posluns (1981), studying women's detailed changes toward freedom from sex-role stereotypes, found that 68% of their changes were deliberate and only 32% "just happened."

I have conducted two small unpublished surveys among graduate students. In one of these, I asked 20 people to list the most important changes in themselves since finishing secondary school, and then to list the most important activities that produced those changes. More than 50% of those activities were highly intentional. In the other survey, I asked 14 people to choose their three largest changes during the past few years. They then categorized 57% of them as intentional, 21% as unintentional, and 21% as uncertain.

Most men who switch to a different career (not just a different job within the same career field) make the change intentionally. Only a few are forced to do so. This finding arose in a study by L.E. Thomas (1977, p. 326). He reported that "there are cases where an individual makes a mid-career change because he is forced to do so by external circumstances. In our sample the few men we found for whom this was true were either technical professionals whose fields were depressed by cutbacks in government funding, or military career men whose failure to receive an expected promotion signaled the necessity for early retirement. In both cases there simply were no other jobs in the same career field available for them to move to."

Even the field of adult socialization is recognizing the major importance of intentional changes. A review chapter on adult socialization (Mortimer and Simmons, 1978, p. 424) has pointed out that "much of adult socialization is self-initiated . . . and voluntary." Furthermore, "failure to take adequate account of the considerable selectivity . . . and self-determination in adult socialization can lead to the excessively conforming 'oversocialized conception of man' . . . that does not allow for innovation, creativity, and change."

A comprehensive study to compare intentional and unintentional changes was in progress as this book went to press. Joan Neehall

(1981) developed an in-depth interview schedule and collected data from 100 adults in Edmonton. Each interviewee was given detailed descriptions of eight areas of change, was given a careful explanation of the distinctions between intentional and unintentional, and was asked what percentage of change in each area over the past four years had been intentional (and what percentage unintentional). In total, 67% of recent change was reported as intentional and only 33% unintentional. In addition, the interviewees rated the intentional portion of their change as far more beneficial than the unintentional portion. For benefits to self and also for benefits to other people, this difference was statistically significant at the .05 level for each of the eight areas of change.

# Chapter 4

# Who Chooses, Plans, and Implements the Changes

With most intentional changes, it is largely the person himself or herself who chooses, plans, and implements the change. Intentional changes are largely "do-it-yourself" changes. The person often obtains significant help from acquaintances, but only rarely from professionals or books.

These insights emerged from our intensive probing interviews with women and men concerning their largest, most significant change during the two years before the interview. Their change had to be definitely, consciously, and voluntarily chosen and intended, though it could be fairly broad rather than foreseen precisely and in great detail.

They were asked who performed each of three major tasks: (1) choosing, (2) planning, and (3) achieving the change. The first task was described in more detail as "deciding to go ahead with this particular change. As part of making this decision, you or someone else or a book might have examined various aspects of your life, obtained information, identified a tentative possible change, estimated the costs and benefits of this change, and so on." The second task was "planning the strategy and deciding the steps for achieving the change." The third was "actually taking the steps for achieving the change."

A handout sheet (sheet #4 in the Appendix) gave the person those descriptions of the three tasks and a list of six possibilities for who might have performed each task. For each task in turn, the person was asked, "How would you divide the credit or responsibility for performing this task? That is, what percentage of the task was performed by you, and what percentage by each of the others in the list?"

The word *steps* is almost as suitable as the word *tasks*. But I rejected *steps* because this word could suggest a simple neat linear path: first the person chooses the change, then plans the strategy, and finally implements the change. The actual picture is quite different: each task may have to be performed many times at various stages of the change effort.

The findings shown in table 4 point up the central position of the person in his or her intentional changes. On the average, the person assumes about 70% of the responsibility for all the subtasks involved in choosing the change, planning the strategy, and implementing the change.

A significant but smaller role is played by friends, family, neighbors, coworkers, and other nonprofessionals during one-to-one interaction. On the average, interviewees gave such persons 23% of the credit for the various steps involved in choosing the particular change, 19% for planning the strategy, and 16% for implementation. In choosing the change, for example, the interviewee may have performed most of the effort of gathering information, weighing alternatives, and making a decision but may have relied on a spouse or friend to add some useful information, suggest other alternatives, and confirm the tentative decision. An interviewee would be considered as performing 100% of the task only if he or she performed the entire task without any help, information, useful advice, or encouragement from anyone else.

The other types of resources in table 4 were used infrequently and contributed relatively little in performing the three tasks. My predictions before the interviews were too high for these categories, and far too low for the person himself or herself. I was especially surprised by the finding that "books, booklets, magazines, television, films, tapes, phonograph records" contributed only about 3%.

## The Central Importance of the Person

We have seen in table 4 that the person herself or himself received a large portion (about 70%) of the credit for choosing, planning, and implementing the changes.

**Extent to Which Various Resources Contributed to
Choosing, Planning, and Implementing the Changes**

| Resource | Choosing | Planning | Implementing |
|---|---|---|---|
| The person himself or herself | 68 | 69 | 73 |
| Nonprofessionals | | | |
| In individual one-to-one interaction | 23 | 19 | 16 |
| In a group | 2 | 2 | 1 |
| Professionals | | | |
| In individual one-to-one interaction | 3 | 7 | 6 |
| In a group | 0.3 | 1 | 2 |
| Books and other nonhuman resources | 4 | 4 | 2 |

Note: For each of the three tasks in turn, each interviewee distributed 100 percentage points among the various resources. This table presents the means of those percentages.

**Table 4**

This percentage is remarkably similar to the percentage of intentional adult *learning* that is planned by the learner himself or herself, rather than by a group, friend, teacher, and so on. A review of research on learning projects found that 73% were self-planned (Tough, 1979, postscript). The closeness of these two percentages is all the more remarkable when one considers that intentional changes are much broader than learning projects, and that the two percentages were derived in quite different ways. For each intentional change, the person reported the percentage of responsibility or credit for each of the categories (self, nonprofessionals, etc.) for each of three tasks; for each learning project, however, the person simply chose the one category into which the planning fitted best.

Parallel findings have also been reported by several other researchers and practitioners. Bolles (1980), for instance, has pointed out that the majority of job changes occur through the person's own efforts and networks rather than through personnel officers, job placement professionals, or newspaper advertisements.

In Veroff's opinion (1978), the data from a 1976 national survey suggest that people now (compared to a similar 1957 survey) have an increased sense of being able to take their life into their own hands and are becoming more confident about their capacities to handle their lives.

Albert Ellis (1977, pp. 6–8) has pointed out that various self-help methods, used without professional supervision, have been very widely used for thousands of years. This may be especially true in the field of religious values or religious therapy. Here are his words:

> In almost all parts of the world, in fact, more people have probably profoundly affected their own lives by do-it-yourself religious therapy than by all other forms of supervised psychotherapy combined. . . . The history of religious therapy almost certainly shows that large numbers of people can bring about profound personality and behavioral changes in themselves by resorting to unsupervised self-help procedures.
>
> In other fields, too, people have read, taken courses, listened to lectures, used films and slides, and utilized many other kinds of self-help devices to aid their lives. . . . I would dare to guess that for every living person who has been helped by formal supervised psychotherapy, ten or more have significantly changed their lives by informal, unsupervised therapeutic modalities. . . .
>
> Innumerable people have testified that, as a result of reading a book, hearing a sermon, viewing a film, or attending a course or a revival-type meeting they have given up alcohol or drugs, stopped smoking, put an end to their feelings of depression, started to forgive rather than to hate their enemies, radically altered their lifestyle, and otherwise made profound changes in their thinking, emoting, and behaving. I have personally talked with or received long letters from literally hundreds of people who have achieved a much less guilty and more enjoying sex life from reading my books . . . and I have spoken with or received written communications from well over a thousand individuals, including many who had been diagnosed by a

psychiatrist as being psychotic, who felt that they had immeasurably improved, and in many instances changed almost the entire tenor of their lives, by reading one of my books on emotional health.

Richard DeCharms (1976, p. 206) has described the behavior of the person who is well able to achieve his or her desired changes. Such behavior seemed characteristic of many, probably most, of our interviewees. DeCharms contrasts such a person (an Origin) with a Pawn, as follows: "The Pawn feels pushed around by external forces because he has not chosen his own path and charted his course through those forces. The Origin may be no more objectively free of the external forces, but he does not allow them to determine his ultimate goals. *He* determines the goals and within the meaningful context of *his* goals he constantly strives to mold the external forces to help him attain his goals. The difference between an Origin and a Pawn does not lie in a personal feeling of freedom vs. constraint. True, the Pawn feels constrained and complains about it. When asked, the Origin may report equal feelings of constraint, but he is not obsessed with them. What is most important in his life is responsible commitment. He strives to visualize his path through the external constraints to the goals that result from his commitment."

As the interviews progressed for this book, the central importance of the person in his or her own change process became very clear. People usually serve as the manager or navigator of their own intentional changes. They may receive advice, encouragement, and information from other people and books, but they fit this help into their own ongoing self-managed process. The person considers various needs and options and strategies, chooses the most appropriate ones, and carries out the steps necessary for achieving the change. The person is an active agent in managing and guiding the process of major change. Like a cross-country runner who encounters various obstacles or a helmsman encountering shoals and storms, the person steers an appropriate course around or through the obstacles. Like the director of a play or the composer and conductor of a symphony, the person seeks an appropriate balance among various components. There are also parallels at the societal level: futurists and policymakers study various options for the future, assess the consequences of each, and then make an informed choice.

The picture that I have just presented emerges clearly by the end of most intensive, probing, leisurely interviews. The stereotype at the beginning of the interview, however, is often quite different.

That, for me, is one of the most fascinating observations to emerge from our interviews. People *believe* that they and others change without much thought, planning, purpose, choice-making, time, and effort. One man said, "Change just happens by accident or else it's caused by others. There's not much *I* can do about it." People are remarkably self-deprecating about their efforts, power, competence, and success at choosing and bringing about major changes in themselves and their lives. Many people feel their pattern is strange or unique, and therefore do not consider it normal and effective and do not discuss it with others.

By the end of a careful thought-provoking interview, however, a quite different picture emerges. People realize they proceeded far more thoughtfully and purposefully than they had initially believed, with carefully chosen, well-organized steps for achieving the change. People are surprised to discover their own planning process, competence, power, and success.

Helping people see their own power and efforts more accurately may be highly beneficial for them. Rodin (1978), for example, has seen definite medical benefits result from simply helping older people see their actual and potential control and effects in their old-age home. The experiment improved their health, not by changing their environment but simply by changing their awareness of their own power and control.

I have been emphasizing the person's conscious, active, initiating, aware, competent part in bringing about changes. It is also true that many external events and forces and changes are beyond the person's control: social norms, government actions, mass media, and other stimuli from the social and physical environment. These external pressures simply happen or exist, regardless of any decision or effort by the person. It is also true that the person's subconscious stream of events rushes onwards as though it had a direction or path of its own. For certain research and practice, it is quite appropriate to focus on the power and control exerted by these external and subconscious forces. In other research and practice, though, it is appropriate to focus on the person's conscious, active, deliberate efforts to choose and change. It is not a case of which view or focus is correct and which is wrong: each of the three is right for some individuals or situations. However, my observation is that too many social scientists and professional helpers have neglected or scoffed at the person's own power and competence in bringing about major changes. They simply have not realized how thoughtful, initiating, and successful people are in their changes.

There are also social scientists who discount the person's power, control, and initiative in another way. They write as though the person's change behavior simply follows a standard pattern that we can study, describe, and predict. Everyone (or at least everyone in a particular category or type) follows the same sequence or the same standard cognitive or information-processing pattern. My own observation is that the person's intentional change process is more idiosyncratic and unpredictable than such writers suggest.

Many policymakers, planners, administrators, economists, historians, and futurists are blind to the person's natural process of change. They are simply not in touch with the total reality. They focus their attention on the highly visible: large-scale institutional and governmental programs, bureaucracies, professional helping enterprises, laws and regulations, public funding. They neglect the underside, the invisible submerged portion of the iceberg, the way things really happen. This underside is often far larger and more pervasive than the highly visible overside.

Elise Boulding (1976, 1979b) has pointed out that this is true in the fields of health care, welfare, education, and food production. These phenomena occur largely at home during our daily lives. Health care delivery systems are involved in only a small fraction of our total effort to maintain our own health and that of our family members. Welfare agencies are usually not part of the process that people go through in solving their problems and obtaining help from peers. Boulding (1979b, p. 12) estimates that, until the end of the fourth grade, mothers give their children considerably more instruction time than teachers do.

In the field of religion, we often think only of the work of the institutional church or synagogue instead of paying attention to the person's own spiritual practices, religious development, ministry, and witnessing. When thinking of research and development, we sometimes think only of officially funded projects and institutions, and forget about the discoveries and inventions made by advanced amateurs in their garages and basements. With couples, we are sometimes more interested in whether the couple is legally married than in the commitment and emotional tone of their relationship. In adult learning we think only of the learning that occurs in courses and classes, which turns out to be only 10% of all intentional adult learning (Tough, 1979). I once had a student loudly proclaim in class that only external things, such as mortgages and traffic jams, are real, and that those of us discussing meditation and spiritual experiences were not in touch with reality. In the 1970s, we sometimes fell for the legal and newspaper view of marijuana and forgot about its remarkably widespread use by a variety of people as a pleasant social activity.

In his chapter on the rise of the prosumer, Toffler (1980) has documented a dramatic shift toward handling our own projects and problems instead of paying someone else to do so. This shift is demonstrated by a sharp increase in the number of medical instruments and kits sold for home use, in the percentage of self-serve service stations, and in the proportion of electric power tools and building materials sold to do-it-yourselfers rather than to carpenters and other professionals. Toffler has also pointed out that most economists ignore all the unpaid work done directly by people for themselves, their families, and their communities; they contemptuously dismiss such work because it is outside of the highly visible market economy. As long as politicians and experts continue to ignore the less visible economic productivity, "they will never be able to manage our economic affairs" (p. 284).

Not only with intentional changes, but with all fields, it is important to look beneath the highly visible surface and to see the total broad phenomenon through the eyes and daily life of the person. Only by understanding the natural process of intentional change, health care, learning, and producing can professionals and governments provide effective help. It is necessary for all of us to escape from the great social lie pointed out by Roszak (1977, p. 30): "The lie insists the tribe, the state, the law, the king, the pharaoh, the party, the general will, the nation is *everything,* while each of us in the privacy of our personal vocation is a wholly dispensable nothing." Planners, decision-makers, administrators, and professionals are often oblivious to the underside, unfortunately, or take it for granted and attach no significance to it.

Let's pause for a moment, at this stage, to try to avoid certain misconceptions. I am simply saying that many adults do, in fact, choose and plan much of their intentional change on their own, with some help from friends and neighbors. This is a natural process, a normal way to handle certain problems, goals, aspects of life, and situations. I am not saying it is the only way: it is just as natural (though not nearly as common) for a person to get help from a professional. There is nothing particularly praiseworthy about one path compared with the other. I am not saying that people necessarily handle their own changes better than a professional would; sometimes they do, but sometimes they do not. What I am saying strongly is this: professionals, researchers, and people themselves have unduly neglected and ignored the thoughtfulness, competence, and success with which many people choose and change. We should shift the balance, and give increased attention and money to research and practice focused on the person as a conscious active agent in change.

## How the Person Chooses the Change

The central importance of the person in his or her own changes is now clear. As we saw in table 4, the person is responsible for about 70% of the various subtasks required for (1) choosing the change, (2) planning the strategy, and (3) implementing or achieving the change. In this section and the next two sections, we turn to the details of those three tasks. What does the person *do* while performing each of the three tasks? What is the person's natural process for making intentional changes?

One major task that the person faces is deciding whether to go ahead with the particular change being considered. That task is examined in this section.

The person is often very thoughtful and active in considering and tentatively choosing some major change, and then in deciding definitely to proceed with it. It is common, for example, for people to examine, reflect on, and assess various facets of themselves and their lives. These facets include their values, goals, hopes, needs, characteristics, lifestyles, knowledge, skill, performance, success, time or money budget, psychological and emotional functioning, physical functioning, and spiritual level. Such an examination can uncover a latent interest, a readiness for change, a deep dissatisfaction, a large gap between the actual and the ideal, a general problem or issue, or a desire to change.

An opportunity, a triggering stimulus, or a change in the external world will often play a part in fostering this self-examination. A situation may deteriorate, for instance: a job, one's weight, an aging parent's health, or the amount of nighttime noise. (In our interviews, these four examples led respectively to a new job, a dieting program, arranging for the interviewee's father to move from the interviewee's household to a nursing home, and moving from an apartment to a daughter's house.) A biography, movie, emotional situation, or conversation may trigger consideration of a particular change, such as having a child or changing jobs. Alternatively, an opportunity may suddenly present itself. A British woman told us that "fate decreed that I buy the BBC magazine the very week a teachers' course was advertised: as a result I enrolled and earned my teaching certificate." Bicycling past a four-plex one morning, a Canadian woman noticed a "for sale" sign in the front yard. Already interested in buying one of the scarce four-plexes in her neighborhood, the woman promptly proceeded to buy this one.

The amount of time and thought and effort that goes into a decision to change varies from a few minutes to a few years. Some changes *could* be decided quickly and without thought, but instead the person explores carefully in order to make a good decision. You could take just a few moments, for instance, to decide to quit your job, move, separate from your spouse, or apply for a degree program—or to do all four simultaneously! To increase your chances of future happiness and health, however, you might well spend many hours reflecting on these possible choices.

Reasoning, thinking, and writing are often an important part of that process. The person may gather information and opinions, list fears and risks, predict the consequences of the potential change, estimate the costs and benefits of the various options, assign weights to the various factors, and set priorities. Before deciding to become pregnant, for example, one woman made a list with two columns for the advantages and disadvantages of having a child. Another woman, describing her decision to switch from being a journalist to becoming a radio producer, said, "I used a balance sheet to figure out the pros and cons of changing jobs."

At suppertime on the day I drafted this section, I discussed it with my daughter. She had recently completed an intentional change that was unusually large for a 14-year-old. She had decided to move from living with one parent to living with her other parent, at least for a few months. I discovered that she had, while considering this change, made a careful list of the pros and cons with the help of her girl friend. My daughter pointed out that the list contained more disadvantages to moving than advantages, but the advantages won out because some of them were particularly strong or large.

Many of us have a mental list of desirable changes in ourselves and our lives. Because we cannot possibly find the time and money to implement all of these desired changes, we must somehow set priorities to choose only two or three at a time. For myself, I have adopted a rather unusual strategy. On the first day of each month, I select a maximum of one change that I will begin that month. I try to avoid any other intentional changes costing more than five hours or $300. This arrangement forces me to choose thoughtfully from among the various possibilities. The large number of possible change paths facing each of us is captured in the movie called *The Man Who Skied Down Everest*. After depicting Yuichiro Miura's heroic feat, the film closes with these lines from his journal: "The end of one thing is the beginning of another. I am a pilgrim again."

In addition to lists and other rational thought, the process of considering and choosing change can include other forms of thought such as fantasy or reflection. The person may vividly imagine one or more alternatives to the present reality and to its normal future extrapolation. Several people whom I know fairly well go even further. For days they will talk and act as though they are almost certain to make a particular change in the near future. But then it turns out that living as though the change is really going to occur is simply their way of testing its fit, and they often drop the idea with no difficulty or regret.

Sometimes a specific method of tapping inner wisdom is used. These methods help people discover their own deepest or highest insights and intuition and knowledge, sometimes illuminating the decision with great clarity. Some changes are first considered or tentatively "chosen" by the subconscious mind: then the task of the person's conscious awareness is to discover these subconscious events and to decide whether to act on them. People use various methods to make contact with their subconscious stream of events or their creative inner wisdom. They work with their dreams, let their thoughts roam freely when awakening in the morning, keep a journal or experiment with free-flowing writing, pray, note unusual behavior (saving money, for example, for no apparent reason, and then realizing their subconscious mind wants a new car or house), use guided fantasies and mind games for discovering an archetypal guide or advisor such as one's wise old man (Masters and Houston, 1972), interpret the *I Ching*, or consult their imaginary doctor (Samuels and Bennett, 1973).

The first time we discussed this topic in my graduate course on personal change paths, two students described how they rely heavily on their subconscious. For a major decision such as getting married or choosing surgery for his child, one man collected the needed data first, but then he waited until meditation and prayer confirmed his decision. Another person, facing a major choice, goes deep into her subconscious and there meets God and finds the needed wisdom.

Sometimes a dream, or series of dreams, can lead to or significantly influence a major personal change. P.F. Thomas (1978) interviewed 40 men and women who were able to describe such an experience. Three-quarters of them found that more than 20 hours of waking time elapsed before the meaning and personal implications of the dream became clear. In order to understand the personal meaning of their dream, the interviewees took such steps as writing down the dream, gestalting it, reflecting on it alone or with other people, writing poetry, reliving the dream, and recalling what they had read earlier about dreams.

Now that we have examined some of the detailed steps involved in choosing the goal, we are better prepared to answer a common question about intentional changes. Some people ask, "Wouldn't you say that the person *always* chooses the change goal himself or herself? The person should always get 100% of the credit for this task." It is true that the person ultimately makes the final decision about whether to proceed with the change. In fact, my definition of intentional changes emphasizes that they must be voluntary to be considered intentional. During the process of making that ultimate decision, however, various resources may be very important with certain subtasks or detailed steps. A person, group, or book could suggest the change in the first place, give the person a fresh perspective on his or her life and characteristics, help the person clarify needs and options. Such a resource could contribute a large amount to the overall task by aiding several of its component subtasks. We emphasized this point in the interview schedule (question #7 in the Appendix): "How would you divide the credit or responsibility for performing this task? That is, what percentage of the task was performed by you, and what percentage by each of the others in the list? I'm not just thinking of who actually made the final decision. No, what I'm thinking of is who or what played some part in the process of assessing the possible change, weighing its consequences, and so on. For instance, a *magazine* might have been very helpful by getting you to see that such a change really would be possible for you."

## How the Person Plans the Strategy

In addition to choosing the change and deciding definitely to proceed with it, the person also has to plan an effective strategy for achieving the change. These two tasks may be intertwined: before deciding to proceed with the change, the person may tentatively choose the strategy and estimate its costs and risks.

Although both tasks must be performed near the beginning of

the entire change effort, they may also be performed several additional times as the effort proceeds. For instance, the person may have to decide whether continuing with this change is worth the costs, or whether or not this particular strategy is turning out to be effective.

Let us turn now to the detailed steps involved in planning the strategy. While planning the initial broad strategy, the person may gather information and advice on various possibilities. This stage could involve weeks of exploration or simply ten minutes of thought. The result will be an initial tentative choice of broad strategies, paths, or resources.

I am struck by the wide variety of techniques, approaches, psychologies, learning principles, and learning styles that the same person will use from one change to another. One key to successful changes may be the person's wide repertoire of strategies from which to choose in particular situations. When a man is trying to change his smoking or eating habits, for instance, he may use a behavior graph, positive and negative reinforcement, control of his environment, and other components of behavior modification. Then when the same man decides to expand his consciousness, he may turn to techniques more typical of humanistic or transpersonal psychology, such as meditation, exercises during trance or hypnosis (Masters and Houston, 1972), or even a psychedelic chemical. When he wants to buy a new house or car, he may gather a great deal of factual information about it in order to make the best choice. When he wants to improve his relationship with his spouse, additional techniques and principles will be useful.

Once the broad initial strategy has been chosen and the change effort is well under way, the need for further strategy decisions may arise. At various times the person may evaluate the current strategy and assess progress and then decide whether to continue, switch to another strategy, drop the change effort prematurely, or stop the effort because it has achieved the desired change. The strategy may be producing certain unanticipated side effects, and the person must decide whether these are beneficial, barely acceptable, or overwhelmingly undesirable. The person may also have to decide how to deal with the various difficulties and problems that arise.

At various points in the process, the person may consider temporarily turning over the planning to someone or something else. The person may decide to follow, for an hour or a year, the strategy decisions of a particular instructor, therapist, medical doctor, consultant, lawyer, group, organization, book, program, or setting.

Usually the person will continue to monitor the effectiveness of that choice and will change to another strategy or resource if necessary. At present, for example, I literally put myself in the hands of a shiatsu masseur for an hour each week. At this stage I do not really know whether the treatments are effective, but after the sixth session, I will assess progress and decide whether to continue.

## How the Person Implements the Change

In order to obtain the desired change, one must not only plan, but also successfully implement, the chosen strategies. One must actually take certain steps in order to achieve the change. Doing this is the third major task.

For some chosen changes, planning and implementing the strategy are quick and easy tasks. Suppose someone decides to drop bowling and spend more time at photography, to accept an attractive unsolicited job offer, to become legally married in a standard civil ceremony, or to have a child. The strategy is simple to plan, and the change is probably easy to achieve.

Other changes require a great deal of insightful planning and difficult implementation. Most notorious of all, for difficulty of implementation, is the effort to break a habit such as smoking, drinking, eating too much, picking one's nose, putting down one's spouse or child, or driving a car too fast. It is easy enough to choose such a change, but hard to achieve it. As many smokers say, "I'm an expert at quitting smoking; I've done it often!" Successfully breaking a habit may require an assortment of self-administered rewards and punishments, along with certain environmental changes such as not allowing cigarettes or beer or sweet foods to enter the house.

Some efforts to break a habit, and many other types of changes, require a series of highly deliberate learning episodes (Tough, 1979). In fact, I estimate that about 30% of all intentional changes involve such a learning effort. For example, the person may want to gain certain skills or knowledge, learn new job responsibilities, change within a close relationship, gain self-insight, perform adequately in a new sport or hobby, play a musical instrument, become physically fit through jogging, increase reading or speaking ability, or gain in understanding the world. The implementation stage for each of these examples would probably involve a series of episodes in which the person's major intention was to gain and retain certain knowledge, skill, or other mental and physical changes. The methods could include reading, listening, practicing, observing, and reflecting.

Other sorts of implementation efforts, too, may be required for certain changes. The person may spend a great many hours trying to find an appropriate job and applying for it. The person may have to persuade other people to allow the desired change or to cooperate with it. Some effort might be required to find a suitable home, car, equipment, support group, partner, club, or doctor.

Finding the time and energy needed for the change can be one step toward implementation. Interviewing 100 persons who had requested an early version of my *Expand Your Life*, Vida Stanius and I asked them, "What interferes with making changes, with controlling your life as much as you'd like to?" Many of the interviewees stated that the demands of their job, their spouse's job, or their children limited their freedom to change.

Gathering up one's courage is necessary for some changes. After interviewing 12 persons for an unpublished study, James Leonidas selected this as one major element in all 12 changes. He said, "People were bold or dramatic; they stepped out; they took a leap for themselves. People in their different ways gathered up their courage to do something new for themselves. In ordinary and everyday ways, all the people I interviewed were quite brave. They all broke new ground for themselves, and were experimenters or pioneers in their own living."

## Nonprofessional Helpers

In the previous section we discussed how the person chooses, plans, and implements the change. We turn now to the major resources used by the person in performing these three tasks. We begin with the most common resource of all: most people give credit to at least one nonprofessional helper. Table 4 showed that nonprofessional helpers contribute far more than the combined total for professionals and nonhuman resources. In fact, they contribute 68% of all external help.

The person gains most nonprofessional help in one-to-one interaction with the helper, and only a small amount (approximately 2% compared to 19%) in groups that meet without a professional helper. Peer groups, mutual support groups, self-help groups, and autonomous learning groups are unquestionably important, but they form only the highly visible tip of the iceberg. Most nonprofessional help is much more casual or hidden below the surface, not structured into weekly meetings of a specific group. As a result, some researchers and practitioners are now focusing on mutual support networks and natural helpers in the community ("socially indigenous help" or "natural helpers") rather than exclusively on groups.

Most of the nonprofessional helpers are family members and friends. Some are coworkers, acquaintances, bartenders, hairdressers, or even strangers.

The helper may contribute to an intentional change in various ways. He or she may suggest or affirm or encourage a particular change, help the person discover a blind spot, agree to cooperate with the change effort and the outcome, warmly encourage the person through the roughest times, suggest strategies and resources for achieving the change or for dealing with obstacles, provide reinforcement for the person according to a behavioral change contract, give the person more time for the change by taking over certain responsibilities, drive the person somewhere, help move furniture, or give the person money. Patterson (1978) reported that natural helpers provide humor, help the person relax, verbalize sympathy and concern, touch and hold, tell about their own experiences and problems, refer to religion and the Bible, and provide companionship. For implementing the change of having a child, two different interviewers on two sides of the Atlantic Ocean put an exclamation mark after "50%: husband."

Not everyone is helpful, of course. Some family members may be threatened by the impending change and may try to sabotage or squelch it. A few acquaintances, even those who are motivated to help, may, in fact, do more harm than good. The question of whether most amateur help is useful, neutral, mixed, or damaging is a major controversy today in several professional fields, such as mental health and social work. One leader (Pancoast, 1978) in the field of natural helping replied to this question as follows: "At this point, I can only report that every professional I have talked with who has become involved with natural helpers, even if initially skeptical, has become convinced of the worth and importance of the natural helpers' services." Some professionals are also quick to assume that giving amateurs some professional training would improve their help, but other professionals believe the opposite. Some types of professional training programs would be more likely to destroy effectiveness than to improve it. Patterson (1978) has also pointed out that a person who is already important and helpful in a friend's life would not necessarily be helpful with a stranger.

Although obtaining help is remarkably common, it may also be difficult, at least for some persons and some changes. If the change involves a basic feeling of inadequacy, or involves the "heavy" emotions of separation, the person may find it hard to approach someone for help. Some people also feel one down after seeking help and believe they can never repay the helper. Most of us, when we want help, will choose a person with whom we feel comfortable, a person whom we can trust, a person who is warm and empathic.

In one field after another, researchers have found that people often gain from someone similar to themselves, rather than from a professional change agent or the mass media (though these are sometimes important).

One such field is the diffusion of innovation. Many studies of people learning about and adopting innovations have demonstrated the significance of nonprofessionals (Rogers and Shoemaker, 1971).

Let us turn next to the field of mental health and personal problems. In a 1976 national survey reported by Antonucci, Kulka, and Douvan (1978), people were asked, "If something is on your mind that is bothering you or worrying you and you do not know what to do about it, what do you usually do?" Compared to 25% in a similar 1957 survey, 35% of the interviewees sought informal social support. The authors described this increase as "dramatic, especially in light of the fact that there is no concomitant change in the degree to which formal support was sought." Of all the first-mentioned helpers, 65% were spouse and other family members, 24% were friends and neighbors, 2% were other acquaintances, and 8% were professionals and specialists. The survey 19 years earlier had found a similar pattern: the respective percentages were 71, 12, 4, and 8, with 5% not ascertained (Gurin, Veroff, and Feld, 1960, p. 368). Of all the studies of how people handle problems and mental health matters, this was one of the earliest to proceed by asking them directly, instead of viewing the phenomenon exclusively through the eyes of professionals. The 1978 authors noted that "despite an apparent increase in the visibility and availability of formal social supports over the last 20 years, there seems to be no overall change in the number or types of formal social supports consulted in response to the kinds of worries and unhappiness tapped by these questions."

Also in the field of mental health, Pancoast (1978) has stated:

> Currently there seems to be a good deal of interest in
> the mobilization of informal community supports as part
> of a broad strategy of prevention and treatment in

community mental health. The recommendations of the President's Commission on Mental Health, which include a heavy emphasis on identifying and strengthening community support systems and natural helping networks, will undoubtedly increase the exposure of mental health professionals and politicians to these ideas. While community support systems should not be viewed as a panacea, and should not be seen as a substitute for professional services, they do have the potential for meeting needs which the formal systems are unable to address.

It seems to me that The Commission Report signals the acceptance of the importance of community supports and that we need no longer be advocates. What is needed now is to pool what we already know about informal community support systems and networks in order to decide on issues which deserve further research and to develop ways of interacting productively with them.

The women's movement to reduce sex-role stereotypes in attitudes and behavior has proceeded largely through nonprofessionals. Home (1978) studied women's changes through consciousness-raising groups. At her doctoral oral exam, she pointed out that much of the relevant activity and change occurred between meetings and after the group had disbanded, largely through peer relationships and reading. The women interviewed by Posluns (1981) used nonprofessionals more than other resources.

Although he did not include women's consciousness-raising groups, Farquharson (1975) discovered a remarkable range of self-help groups. They were effective not only in helping the person deal with the initial problem (such as drinking, gambling, weight, physical handicap, bereavement, child-raising), but also in improving self-confidence in the ability to relate to other people effectively and helpfully. Conversations with Andy Farquharson brought the phenomenon of mutual support in helping networks to my attention and raised the possibility that these networks often wither or collapse when a professional moves in.

The importance of nonprofessionals is also demonstrated by D. Armstrong (1971, p. 110). He found that the conversion from a person uninterested in learning to a highly motivated and active learner was the result of (1) a chance meeting with a stranger who introduced the person to a new skill or body of knowledge, (2) a friend who invited the person to a concert, lent the person a book, or introduced the person to a fascinating idea, or (3) a relative or friend who encouraged or aided the person's learning, or expressed faith in the person's ability to learn.

Three studies of the major learning efforts of adults have found that self-planned learning (rather than learning in a group or through private instruction) is not a lonely or isolated activity. In fact, I would bet that there is more interaction with more people around the content and the process in self-planned learning than there is in the traditional classroom or course. In the majority of learning efforts, the person retains the overall day-to-day control over what and how to learn, but simultaneously receives plenty of help, encouragement, advice, and information from several other persons. In each self-planned learning project, the adult receives help from a mean of 10.6 individuals, a median of 9.5 (Tough, 1967). Every interviewee in that study used at least four helpers. They were largely acquaintances, friends, and family members. In a replication in the United Kingdom, Strong (1977) found a similar pattern, although her mean was only 7.4 and the median 8. I found that 75% of all helpers were approached on a personal rather than a business basis, and Strong's comparable figure was 79%. Luikart (1977) obtained an average number of helpers remarkably close to mine: 10.3 compared to 10.6. He found that the amount, source, and type of help received by the learners were significantly associated with differences in the size, density, and composition of their personal social networks.

## Professional Helpers

Because I have always earned my living as a professional helper, I am particularly interested in knowing how much contribution professionals make to a person's intentional change. In table 4, then, I am especially interested in the data for people who are paid, employed, designated, or trained to help. In the interviews, we used these words: "a person who was paid to help, or was doing so as part of his or her job, or was designated by some organization to help, or was trained to help." In individual one-to-one interaction, these professional helpers contributed about 5% toward the total responsibility for choosing, planning, and implementing the change. As a leader or speaker or expert in a group situation, they contributed about 1%.

Professional help, then, is clearly not central in the process of most intentional changes. People do use professional help sometimes, and it can be very important and useful when it is used. Many other changes proceed successfully without professional help, however, or with an insignificant amount. In short, professional help is central in a few change projects, present but not central in some others, and not present at all in many.

Relatively little professional help was obtained while choosing the change (table 4). Although twice as much professional help was obtained with the other two tasks, it was still less than one-third of all the help received with those tasks. When one reads most of the literature on major changes, one gets the impression that the phenomenon revolves around a central core of professionally guided approaches, such as psychotherapy, counseling, human growth groups, Gestalt, *est,* encounter, rebirthing, social work, management development, staff training and development, and adult education. Matson (1977) presents an excellent panorama of these methods. But when we listen to the people themselves describe their largest intentional changes, we discover that they often proceed without using these professionally guided methods. Even when they do use a professional helper, they often retain some or much of the responsibility for planning and implementing the change.

The amount of professional help received may be increasing over the years. In the previous section, I referred to a 1976 survey across the United States that was similar to a 1957 survey. Looking at the data on what people do if something is bothering or worrying them, Antonucci and others (1978) found no increase in the number of people (8%) who consult a professional or specialist. However, another report (Kulka, 1978) at the same symposium focused on different data from the same two surveys. Referring to various personal problems, the interviewer said, "Sometimes when people have problems like this, they go someplace for help. Sometimes they go to a doctor or minister. Sometimes they go to a special place for handling personal problems—like a psychiatrist or a marriage counselor, or social agency, or clinic. How about you—have you ever gone anywhere like that for advice and help with any personal problem?" In 1957 only 14% said yes, but that had risen to 26% in 1976.

When one thinks of professional helpers with major changes, one naturally thinks of doctors, psychiatrists, clinical psychologists, counselors, clergy, and social workers. There is no doubt these are all important and relatively common. For instance, most of these professions show up in the data reported by Gurin and others (1960), Antonucci and others (1978), Kulka (1978), and the interviews for this book. Some other persons who are paid or designated to help with changes may surprise us, however, because they do not fit our stereotype of professional helpers. A woman credits the instructor of her diet workshop with a major contribution to her weight loss, for example. Another woman, in the midst of changing her style of interacting with her two teenagers, found one of their teachers very helpful. Two people whose changes were job related gained enormously from a supervisor and personnel manager respectively. My very first interview was with a woman whose largest change was moving to live with a friend: professional movers contributed to this change by moving her heavy furniture from her old apartment to the new one. Several interviewees have mentioned a lawyer or real estate agent as important but not central.

## Books and Other Nonhuman Resources

Books, booklets, magazines, other printed materials, television, films, tapes, cassettes, and phonograph records receive only about 3% of the credit for helping with choosing, planning, and implementing intentional changes (table 4). Does this remarkably low figure fairly represent the actual contribution of books and other nonhuman resources? Surely the landscape and process of intentional change would be dramatically altered if all books, tapes, and television completely disappeared. Many graduate students in my course on personal change paths, after reading 15 books chosen from a 60-item bibliography, report to me that their choices of changes and paths are greatly affected. On the other hand, the low figure is supported by my review of research on intentional learning, which found that only 3% of all adult learning projects were planned or guided largely by books and other nonhuman resources (Tough, 1979, postscript). The low figure is also supported by P.F. Thomas (1978), who found that people gained virtually no help from books and other materials while choosing their change, though they did recall useful insights from their earlier reading. This may be the key: people don't turn to books at the time of the change, but do use ideas from earlier reading. The crowded bookstore shelves and the sales figures for various types of self-help books and cassettes indicate their widespread use.

Many books are designed to help largely with the third task: implementing the change. Just follow the directions in this book or tape and you will become more confident, have a better self-image, raise your children more competently, be a better spouse or lover, become healthier, or whatever. Such books have been available, and presumably useful, for centuries. "During the latter half of the sixteenth century and the beginning of the seventeenth century, printers in London were publishing guides to domestic life, religious handbooks, . . . handbooks on health and medicine, . . . how to cultivate one's memory, needlework, and navigation" (Newsom, 1977, p. 20).

Some books are designed to help people with the difficult tasks of choosing their changes and planning their strategy. A fascinating range of models, each one in its own unique way useful and powerful for certain persons, is provided by the following examples of such books: Bell and Coplans (1976), Bolles (1980), Browne (1973), Coyne and Hebert (1972), Faraday (1976), Grof (1975), R. Gross (1977), Lakein (1973), Matson (1977), G.P. Miller (1978), Naranjo (1972), O'Neill and O'Neill (1974), and Tough (1980). I often urge every institution and professional engaged in facilitating change to display and lend these books to their clients.

Recently I have been following the self-help book *How to Sleep Better* by Coates and Thoresen (1977). Like many other good self-help books, it is an effective mixture of control and freedom. It often takes the reader one step at a time, sometimes very exactly and narrowly. At the same time, the authors urge each of us to "become a personal scientist." Following the book, my first step was to observe and record my own behavior and to keep a sleep diary. This information gave me some hunches about which of their strategies would work best for me, and also suggested how to modify some of their strategies to meet my particular needs and problems. The rest of the book, too, provides an effective balance of detailed step-by-step instructions combined with invitations to select and modify the authors' strategies.

## Variations in the Basic Pattern

In summary, the person himself or herself receives credit for a mean of 70% of the responsibility for choosing, planning, and implementing the change. Family, friends, and other nonprofessionals are responsible for 21%. Professionals account for 6%, and books and other nonhuman resources for 3%. This basic pattern was presented in table 4.

Do these four percentages vary significantly at the .05 level as we look at different demographic groups and other variables? In general the answer is no, using one-way analyses of variance, but a few interesting variations do occur.

Let us look first at the areas of change. The mean percentage for self did not vary significantly. The range was fairly wide, though: the amount of responsibility assumed by the person herself or himself ranged from 59% with religion to 86% with basic competence. Reliance on nonprofessionals varied significantly over the nine areas of change. The mean percentage ranged from 7% with physical health (basic competence and religion were also fairly low) to 23% with relationships, 27% with maintenance, and 32% with residence location. Reliance on professionals did not vary significantly, but it did range from a low of 0.2% with volunteer helping activities to a high of 12% with religion. The contribution of books and other nonhuman resources varied significantly over the nine areas of change. These resources contributed zero in the area of basic competence and 1% with volunteer helping activities contrasted with 7% for enjoyable activities, 9% for physical health, and 17% for religion. Although the mean percentages for both nonprofessionals and books varied significantly over the nine areas of change, no two areas were sufficiently different to be significant, according to the Sheffe statistical procedure for comparing particular groups of data.

Let us turn now to six demographic variables. None of the mean percentages (self, nonprofessionals, professionals, books) varied significantly at the .05 level with age, sex, educational level, social class, or race. Significant differences were found, though, among the three countries for each of self, professionals, and books, but not for nonprofessionals. The interviewees in Canada reported an average of 74% for self, 20% for nonprofessionals, 4% for professionals, and 2% for books and other nonhuman resources. The corresponding percentages for people in England were 69, 14, 8, and 8. In the U.S.A. the percentages were 56, 27, 11, and 6. Despite these significant differences, the basic pattern (rank order) did not vary from one country to another. Although the samples were not chosen to represent the entire nation, and the sample sizes are not large enough to warrant an extended discussion, it is interesting to note that the Americans were particularly low in the credit they gave to themselves, and particularly high in the use of nonprofessionals and professionals.

After the previous paragraph was written, I received additional data from England. Judith Calder, on leave from The Open University in the fall of 1981, interviewed people chosen from the local electoral register for one country town in Buckinghamshire and is writing a paper based on those interviews. She was able to send me the data from her first 25 interviews just before this book went to press. Several of her findings support the findings reported in this book, but two of her percentages differ markedly from the national patterns reported in my previous paragraph. Her mean percentage for self (51%) was even lower than the American percentage, and the figure for nonprofessionals (35%) was even higher than that for the Americans. I hope that nationwide sampling in many countries in the future will illuminate the differences among nations.

Did the contribution of self, nonprofessionals, professionals, or books vary significantly with the five variables described in the previous chapter? Those five variables were size, percentage achieved, extent to which the change was noticed by others, amount of benefit to self, and amount of benefit to others. Multiple regression analyses were used for percentage achieved, and one-way analyses of variance for the other variables. Of the 20 possible relationships, only 3 were significant at the .05 level. Each of these three will be discussed in turn. (1) The mean percentage for self varied significantly with the size of the change. The changing person contributed only 67% to the choosing, planning, and implementing of huge or enormous changes, 64% to fairly large and important changes, 79% to definite changes with some relevance and importance, and 87% to the few changes that were small, trivial, petty, unimportant. (2) The mean percentage for nonprofessionals, too, varied significantly with the size of the change. The four percentages were 24, 23, 14, and 7. (3) Books and other nonhuman resources contributed 5% in changes that were noticed by only 0–5 persons, 8% in changes noticed by 6–10 persons, and only 2% in changes noticed by more than 10 persons.

# Chapter 5

# Implications for Improving Professional Practice and Policy

The overall picture of intentional changes is presented in the first four chapters. We have seen how large, significant, and beneficial these changes are. We have noted the dominant role that people play in choosing, planning, and implementing their own changes. They obtain some help from friends and other nonprofessionals, and less help from professionals and books.

Having seen this comprehensive picture of intentional changes in the first four chapters, we turn now to the implications for improving professional practice and policy. After I present the basic data regarding intentional changes to various professional audiences, the most common question they ask is, "What do you think we should *do* about all this: what are the implications for practitioners?" The question is usually marked by enthusiasm and puzzlement; the person eagerly wants to foster intentional changes but cannot figure out how to proceed.

Over the past few years I have spent a great deal of time thinking through my responses to this question. In fact, I am writing this paragraph at the end of twelve hermit days that I set aside to consider these implications more thoroughly and comprehensively than before. I have selected the seven directions that I consider most significant for action during the next few years. These are the most useful directions for fostering and facilitating beneficial changes. Each significant direction is spelled out in one section of this chapter.

My purpose is to stimulate you to think through for yourself the implications for your particular situation. You might want to take a few minutes right now to jot down your own thoughts about the most significant innovative practices or research projects that could be developed in your own professional field or organization. In the next few months, what might you do differently as a result of your new understanding of intentional changes?

Before tackling that question, you might want to learn more about intentional changes. You could continue reading, for instance, or you could ask a few people to tell you about their recent intentional changes. You could choose your own largest, most important change from all the changes that you have chosen and achieved during the past two years. Ask yourself and the people you interview, "What were the greatest difficulties in choosing and achieving the change? What additional help and resources and competence would have been especially beneficial?" Probe leisurely for insightful answers.

I am often asked why we should become involved at all in trying to facilitate a natural process that is already reasonably successful. "We might mess things up and make them worse for people." It is true that we could blunder in and insensitively do more harm than good. I would rather do nothing at all than harm a reasonably successful activity. If we thoroughly and accurately understand the natural phenomenon before we try to be helpful, however, and if we try to fit into the person's natural process instead of making the person fit into ours, I believe we can be of great benefit. People do have great difficulties with many changes, and themselves say they would benefit from additional help and competence. I believe they are right.

During my two weeks of concentrated thought for this chapter, I read about 4,000 pages of notes on this question that I had made over the years. In addition, my suggestions are based on the interview responses of a wide variety of adults to questions 6A, 9D, 9E, 9F, and 11 in the Appendix. I was also stimulated by parts of McGinnis (1975) and by rereading chapter 9 of Tough (1967).

Within our own portions of the enormous enterprise devoted to helping people change, what can we do? To improve our impact in promoting beneficial and effective changes, here are the seven potential directions that I consider most significant during the next few years:

1. improve individual competence in managing change,
2. develop better help with goals and planning,
3. increase information about opportunities and resources,
4. reduce undue restrictions on freedom of choice,
5. widen the range of opportunities and resources,
6. improve ongoing support from nonprofessionals,
7. improve the effectiveness of professional helpers.

Professional practitioners could experiment immediately with certain directions during their teaching, counseling, or other helping sessions. Graduate students and faculty members could explore several directions in small-scale projects. Leaders in the women's movement and the self-help movement, teachers in free university classes and other informal settings, religious leaders, librarians, and authors could usefully implement several of the directions. High-level policymakers, public officials, and administrators could take steps to study or implement each of these directions.

Each direction is outlined in one of the following sections.

## Improve Individual Competence in Managing Change

One potential direction is to help people become more knowledgeable about intentional changes in general, and more competent in planning their own. The benefits from this direction could be enormous. In my more optimistic moments I envision a far-reaching groundswell of people discovering their own power and success at changing, and as a result changing much more beneficially and effectively.

People are remarkably self-deprecating about their own self-guided change. They are simply not in touch with the variety, competence, and success of their changes, nor with how thoughtful, active, and responsible they are in these changes. They lack confidence in their ability to diagnose a problem or situation, to choose targets and strategies, and to evaluate the results. They feel powerless and incompetent at changing without the help of a professional. People simply do not recognize nor treasure all the change, learning, health care, and problem-solving that they perform on their own and with friends and family. Some people have even reached the point of believing that if change or learning is not conducted or at least certified by a qualified professional, it simply is not legitimate, significant, and worthy. Some people have these false beliefs: "The only way to change successfully is with professional helpers. Only in their hands am I safe, and assured of an effective, acceptable, legitimate path. Change is incredibly difficult, risky, even dangerous if I try it on my own or with uncredentialed helpers."

Many people believe they are strange and unique in how they change. They believe they fail to correspond to some common pattern, even though they cannot articulate what that pattern is. They lack a raised consciousness that "changing on your own, and with peers, is beautiful, effective, normal, and natural." As a result, they may not readily discuss their change process with others as a natural topic of conversation and may thus miss out on encouragement and suggestions.

A low self-image as a changing person and exaggerated faith in the power of professionals can make the person less confident at managing change, less likely to take initiative and responsibility for changes, and less powerful and competent at achieving relevant changes.

As professionals interested in fostering beneficial changes, what can we do to counteract the erroneous beliefs and self-perceptions and to improve individual competence in managing change?

The first step in this direction is to help people gain increased *awareness and knowledge* of intentional changes. Many people are ignorant about their own changes, let alone intentional changes in general, and even have various false assumptions that hinder their changes. Information about the normal natural processes of intentional change could be fascinating and useful for these people. They would be quite surprised by how important and widespread intentional changes are and affirmed by the fact that their changes are mostly do-it-yourself with help from friends and other nonprofessionals. It would also be useful for people to gain accurate knowledge about their own recent change efforts by listing these efforts, noting their paths and difficulties and outcomes. As people come to see the variety of goals and paths for change, they regard their own change efforts more highly. They no longer feel ashamed or worried because of the false belief that their ways of changing are somehow strange or inferior.

It is time to correct the unbalanced picture of change presented by many writers, professional helpers, and television programs. They often depict changes either as unintentional or as professionally guided (or occurring in groups or through preprogrammed materials). Highly intentional, successful, self-guided change with help from nonprofessionals is simply not portrayed very often in fiction, nonfiction, television programs, professional literature, and re-search literature. I wish people would not write about intentional changes before thoroughly understanding them, examining their own change efforts in detail, and interviewing several persons at length about their changes. I do not believe that self-guided changes are somehow better than other kinds, but I do believe they have been neglected in the print and electronic media. The time has come for an accurate balance.

Let me hasten to point out that a few books have already pre-sented a balanced picture of intentional change. Good examples are Bolles (1980), Coyne and Hebert (1972), Faraday (1976), R. Gross (1977), Moustakas (1977), O'Neill and O'Neill (1974), Rogers (1977), Stevens (1971), Tough (1980), and some of the behavioral self-control books. More than 160 years ago, at least one writer emphasized self-guided change and learning, which he called "self-instruction, self-command, self-acting energy" (I. Taylor, 1820, p. 8). Later in the book he exclaimed: "Glorious is the prospect, most fascinating the hope, held out by self-cultivation to those who . . . gather every day and every hour something that shall open the mind to yet greater improvement, prepare for further exertions, and ensure success in studies, and arts, and pursuits, of highest importance, through years long to come" (pp. 87–88).

A second step is to help people *see the effectiveness* of their own natural change process quite accurately. Most people have a very low opinion of their capacity for bringing about changes in them-selves and their lives. They see their failures and mistakes. They see how far they still have to go in their changes, but not how far they have already come. If they examine their personal changes more thoughtfully, they may realize that they are remarkably capa-ble, powerful, and successful at bringing about various changes and at solving problems. They may come to treasure their own change efforts and to see themselves as an origin instead of a pawn (De-Charms, 1976).

The benefits of this new self-image could be far-reaching. After 40 intensive interviews, McGinnis (1975) concluded: "I suspect that the more that adults become aware of the process of personal change and the fact that they do indeed change, the more they will be able to resist undesirable alterations and manage their own per-sonal growth" (p. 197).

John Loughary has developed in some detail the concept of self-empowerment. His unpublished manuscript provided a foundation for a factorial study by Bramucci (1977), and for a workshop approach to increasing the person's self-empowerment and planning skills (developed by Loughary and T. Ripley, and presented in Bramucci, app. I).

A third step is to help people *become even more effective at performing the various tasks and steps* involved in intentional change. Although many people are already performing these tasks reasonably well, my guess is that some of these people and many others could benefit greatly by becoming even more competent, thoughtful, and assertive. Instead of hoarding our professional expertise, we could give it away to anyone who wants it. We will have to be certain, though, that our principles and general suggestions really fit the change process of most adults and are not simply our own style or biased view.

To stimulate your thinking, here are some possible tasks and steps at which people might become more competent: (a) sorting out one's own interests, needs, problems, action goals, preferences, and priorities; (b) establishing the costs and benefits of potential change; (c) setting goals or targets or directions for change, when appropriate, in various areas of life (job, other contributions to society, health, inner personal change, family, human relations, spiritual growth, values, lifestyles, travel, generally having a happy effective life); (d) self-assessment, estimating one's desired level, and seeking and accepting feedback; (e) making the necessary plans, decisions (broad strategy and particular methods), and arrangements; (f) dealing with problems, difficulties, turmoil, sense of loss, pain, unanticipated side effects, and obstacles along the way; (g) obtaining encouragement and support when needed, but avoiding undue influence from the expectations of others; (h) time and money management; (i) actually implementing the change. The last task in that list might require effective reading and listening skills, developing a repertoire of other change techniques, improving one's memory, some basic knowledge of psychological principles, and some grasp of behavioral self-control procedures.

In addition, one-sixth of our interviewees spontaneously reported they would have benefited from additional skills at human relations, communications, and assertiveness. Also, several people mentioned their need for additional motivation, self-discipline, determination, courage, confidence, or physical energy.

As I think about the person who is highly competent at bringing about change, I often picture a long-distance runner or a cross-country motorcycle rider. Confident, determined, proactive, the runner or rider faced with difficult terrain will surmount or bypass each obstacle calmly and competently. In addition, the competent changer of the future may be remarkably thoughtful, reflective, insightful, self-directing, flexible, effective, and joyful. Such persons may seriously consider a wide range of relevant options before narrowing and choosing. They may manage their changes and their lives with good cheer and an easy flair. They may be not only sufficiently thoughtful and goal-oriented, but also sufficiently loose and flowing and open to spontaneous opportunities.

Most people would also benefit from recognizing and cheerfully accepting the 80 or 90% of themselves and their lives that is not going to change. This ability to live cheerfully without certain changes is essential because there is a sharp limit to the amount of change one can successfully achieve. Health, money, or job can make certain changes very unlikely. Three of our interviewees were unable to find a suitable partner for dating, marriage, and travel respectively.

The fourth step is for the person to become *highly effective at getting appropriate help* when needed. People who are competent at managing their changes have to sense when they would benefit from help and when they can do without. Then they have to choose the most useful resources, whether a professional helper, a friend or neighbor, a particular book, or a group. Finally, when faced with that resource, the person must be proactive and skillful in getting the needed help and information.

As people become more aware, thoughtful, and insightful about their own change efforts, they may want to use far more professional services and resources than they do now. If professionals and their materials are flexible enough to fit emerging needs, the demand for them may double or triple as people become more in touch with their change process and its difficulties. The percentages in table 4 for professionals and books might rise dramatically over the next three decades. It is also possible, of course, that the opposite will happen. As people become more knowledgeable and competent in managing their changes, they may use professionals and books even less. It is hard to predict which way this will go, particularly because the outcome will be affected largely by how rapidly and flexibly professionals develop materials and resources that fit into the person's ongoing natural process of intentional change.

**Some Possibilities for Implementation.** As with several later suggestions in this chapter, this first direction could be initiated with a variety of populations. It could be implemented for the general public, for the employees or clients in one organization, for the members of one occupation or union or professional association, or for one neighborhood. It could be provided for the entire range of intentional changes, or it could focus primarily on one area of life, such as health, career, male-female relationships, child-raising, spiritual growth, leisure activities, or time management.

You could experiment with this direction using whatever medium or approach is most suitable for you or your employer. For example, you could write a booklet, newspaper column, magazine article, or book. You could collect and display, lend, or sell any printed materials that are already available. You could consider films, television, radio, and cassette tapes as possibilities. Computers, interactive two-way TV, and other communications media might also be used for this some day. The distant future might also bring newsletters and magazines for those interested in developing their competence at changing and learning, just as magazines now exist for those interested in developing their competence at running, sailing, homemaking, and so on.

It would also be reasonably inexpensive and easy to develop workshops, courses, and peer groups for gaining competence at managing change. A group dealing with "Powerfully Guiding Your Changes" or "How to Manage Your Own Changes" might attract many interested persons.

Knowledge and competence for managing change could also be gained in a one-to-one situation. Information centers, counseling, and everyday conversations might be used. The helper might be a professional, a lay volunteer, or a friend. In fact, one easy approach is simply this: the helper asks the other person to talk for an hour or two about his or her own change efforts. If the helper listens empathically, insights and resolutions may occur spontaneously.

If many of us experiment with various approaches, we will eventually learn which approaches work best for which sorts of people. Feedback and evaluation will enable us to develop even better approaches. Also, as more and more people try to develop their competence at managing change, we will gradually learn just what sorts of improvement are possible, how many people are interested, and what stops others from being interested.

## Develop Better Help with Goals and Planning

Developing better ways of assisting with goals and planning is a second significant direction for action. I consider it so important that I have already spent four years working at it through a funded development project. My hope is that many other people in a variety of situations and occupations will also experiment with this direction. Then, several years from now, we will be in a good position to select the especially effective procedures for various sorts of persons and media.

The purpose is to develop a variety of effective help with choosing goals and directions for change, and with choosing broad strategies and paths. In many of our interviews we asked what was the most difficult part of the entire change process. About 33% of the interviewees indicated they would have benefited from better help with goal-setting and 40% from better help with planning strategy.

Various sorts of help can give the person a clearer context or firmer foundation for assessing and choosing particular directions for change. Some people need exercises or a framework for setting their broad life goals and activities. They may also need to establish an appropriate balance among these goals through a time and money budget. Others need help in clarifying some problem or unsatisfactory area of life, or in clarifying their needs, wants, interests, fantasies, wishes. Many need to develop more accurate self-assessment and self-insight through feedback, simple self-testing and self-diagnostic tools, and exercises that provide people with snapshots of themselves from various angles. To help people see and appreciate their major skills and strengths, Penny Garner (of Taking Charge! in Washington, D.C.) has had people list their recent successful efforts to learn and change.

Each of us is bombarded daily with messages and pressures to change. These come from radio, television, newspapers, magazines, friends, colleagues, employer, spouse, children, and parents. Each of us has to select the changes to consider seriously. To obtain some notion of the number of change messages to which we are exposed, Susan Tough went through just the first section of our local newspaper one day (*Toronto Star*, March 3, 1979). She found 61 news articles and display advertisements that would probably stimulate at least 100 newspaper readers to consider changing. Of these 61 messages, 26 urged a change in product or store, 12 urged improvement of current home or moving somewhere else, 6 urged travel, 6 described a course or lecture, 3 suggested changes in how one does one's job, 3 urged changes in behavior as a parent, 3 proposed a particular recreational activity, and 2 urged conservation of energy or the environment. No wonder Toffler (1980, p. 392) proposed "a cadre of professional and paraprofessional 'life-organizers.' "

For some people, an important foundation for decision-making is their broad perspective on human life gained through studying history, alternative futures, psychic and spiritual literature, or astronomy. Powerful perspective can also be gained by listing one's major intentional changes over the years on a chronological chart. In a sense this involves examining one's own past in order to think about one's future. Another sort of valuable perspective can come from discussing or listing one's entire range of life goals at one sitting.

Several interviewees had a particular change clearly in mind but were uncertain whether to go ahead with it. They would have benefited from encouragement, from general advice, or from more information regarding the potential change and its likely effects on other aspects of their lives. Some people will need to estimate the time and money required for the change, investigate whether that much time and money is available, and decide whether the change would be worth the costs.

Two activities fall somewhere between setting goals and planning one's strategy. One of these is to set a series of immediate changes or subgoals that will eventually lead to the desired change. The achievement of each intermediate goal produces visible progress toward the distant goal, thus providing satisfaction and encouragement. It also gives the person a chance to stop at that point if the distant change loses its appeal as a result of experiencing a portion of it.

The other in-between activity is to survey a broad panorama of possible changes and opportunities. A workshop or television program can perform this function, as can books. Such books have been written by Grof (1975), Lande (1976), Matson (1977), Naranjo (1972), and Tough (1980).

We turn now to the possibilities of better help with planning the strategy for achieving a change. Some people benefit greatly from learning about the vast panorama of available paths and methods (guided by a professional, a peer, or oneself). Others need general advice and information regarding the various broad paths. One person who did not know how to begin a particular change effort said, "I felt overwhelmed and lost at first," and another said, "I was a beginner—and alone—in a complex field." Some need advice on raising money and arranging other logistics. A few interviewees found they had difficulty getting some other person (a family member or a business-relationship person, for example) to agree to the change or to perform certain actions.

A few people needed more help learning to perform the desired behavior (a new job or hobby, for instance) because of the high level of skill that it required. A surprisingly large number of people found themselves in quite a different situation. The new behavior was easy enough to perform—at least for a few minutes or hours. But the person needed greater self-discipline or willpower, or simply to remember. Examples were diet, smoking, and behaving differently in a particular relationship. These people would probably have benefited from learning various principles of behavioral self-control.

Toward the end of the planning process, it is time for the person to set priorities and choose one or two particular directions and paths for change. In my workshops and in *Expand Your Life,* I provide a simple chart for this purpose. It has just two columns, one labeled "What major changes do I want in myself and my life?" and the other "To move toward each change, what steps could I take?" I encourage people to jot down all their high-priority possibilities, and then to see whether any can be combined. The person is then ready to choose one or two for the next few months.

A thoughtful exploration of how to help people set goals and broad strategies for change, effectively manage their changes and the resulting stress, and take advantage of the opportunities embedded in every major transition has been provided by Adams, Hayes, and Hopson (1976, particularly chaps. 1, 11, and 13). *The Adult's Learning Projects,* too, presented some detailed suggestions for help with goal-setting and strategy-planning (Tough, 1979, particularly chaps. 10 and 14).

**Some Possibilities for Implementation.** The first two directions in this chapter could be combined by some helpers or centers. Throughout the process of providing effective help with current tasks, one can also help the person become more competent and confident at making choices and plans independently next time. As a result, more and more people will combine the delightfully effective qualities of a cross-country runner, a highly competent navigator or pilot, and Jonathan Livingston Seagull.

To provide the diversity of help described in this section, we need a variety of approaches and lengths. There should be something available for people of all ages, levels, lifestyles, values, and neighborhoods. There should be something available for the person with just a simple quick question, something for the person who wants to go through a thorough 120-hour self-exploration, and something for all those in between. There should be a variety of approaches and content available to fit the great variety of needs and individual differences.

Some of the help with goals and strategy will be aimed at the general public in one nation (a book) or region (a workshop or a counseling center). Some services will be aimed at one particular area of life, such as career, education, or human relationships. Other services will be aimed at one particular target population, such as women, managers, employees of one organization or department, parents, politicians, teachers, some other occupation or profession, or students enrolled in one educational institution or program.

Services might be offered by a variety of agencies. Public libraries, Y's, community centers, boards of education, colleges and universities, human growth centers, counseling and mental health centers, adult education agencies, staff development departments, professional associations, career and life-planning centers, educational brokering, and educational information centers are all possibilities. (However, I worry a little about help with goals and strategies being lodged in an organization that itself provides courses, programs, or other change paths. There is such a strong temptation to slant the "help" toward having the person choose that organization's own courses or programs.)

A movement called "assessment centers" might develop in a similar direction, according to the authors of an *Annual Review of Psychology* article. "Such centers are perhaps becoming environments for both assessment and personal development. In an increasingly bureaucratic and impersonal world, assessment (including self-assessment) centers and similar community outreach programs may become more common in helping people get in touch with themselves and in assisting them with life changes, lifelong learning, and general enhancement of coping skills and quality of life" (Sundberg, Snowden, and Reynolds, 1978, p. 208).

A comprehensive and highly integrative study by Cross (1978) suggests that the field of lifelong learning may increasingly become involved in helping adults set goals and plan strategies. The major need pointed out by many research studies and blue-ribbon panels, according to Cross, is counseling services (and printed materials or computer programs) to help people learn about themselves and about available opportunities, plan their own learning strategies, and find appropriate resources. Here is her resounding summary (p. 43): "The goal of the learning society is to make adults stronger, better-informed, more self-directed learners; it is not to make learners increasingly dependent on others to tell them what, when, where and how to learn. Educators have a vital role to play in this effort. Research indicates that adult learners do want and need help. In particular, they need help in planning and utilizing learning activities that will help them to reach their goals. One of the greatest needs in a society with a rich variety of learning resources and a potential constituency of millions is to make the necessary connections between learners and resources. If that 'missing link' can be supplied, the learning society can become a reality."

As with the first direction, this second one can be pursued through three main channels: print and other materials, group programs, and one-to-one interaction. Let us turn first to books and other printed materials.

Government printers, public libraries, and bookstores handle countless books and booklets on how to grow vegetables, care for children, repair your home, and cook—but not on how to choose and guide your total range of changes. Printed tools for their clients could be usefully produced or bought (and given, lent, or sold) by virtually any helping professional or agency. Agencies and centers that choose not to display or lend these materials could at least provide an annotated bibliography for their clients. For example, I often hand out a list called "Useful Books for Choosing and Guiding Your Learning and Change." It includes such items as Bolles (1980), Browne (1973), Crystal and Bolles (1974), Ford and Lippitt (1976), R. Gross (1977), Lakein (1973), Loughary and Ripley (1976), Naranjo (1972), O'Neill and O'Neill (1974), Scholz and others (1975), Simon (1974), and Tough (1980). When Vida Stanius and I checked with people who had been sent an early mimeographed form of Expand Your Life, we found that 2 people had barely glanced at it, 16 had read it carefully or completely but recalled little or no effect, and 8 people reported some definite effect or change produced by the book.

Simple printed tools for diagnosis and for ranking the available options could usefully be produced by every professional helper and center. For example, the Ontario Society for Training and Development (1979) has published a 29-page self-rating list of skills and knowledge needed by instructors, designers, managers, and consultants. Diagnostic self-assessment kits for use by dentists, pediatricians, psychiatrists, and other professionals in discovering their areas of relative weakness and ignorance have been described by T.B. Friedman (1978).

Perhaps the day is not far away when this significant direction will also be facilitated by certain newspaper and magazine articles, television and radio programs, cassette tapes, and interactive computer programs.

Workshops and courses are another inexpensive way of providing better help. Group programs ranging from one hour to three weeks could be very useful in encouraging and helping both goal-setting and strategy-planning. The stimulating and supportive presence of other members can be very beneficial.

I have led two-hour and one-day workshops for the general public on "Choosing Your Paths for Personal Change." At first we do various exercises (described in Tough, 1980) to increase self-insight concerning goals, values, hopes and wishes for the future, and so on. Then we survey the various available paths and nearby places. Finally, each participant lists possibilities and then narrows them down to one or two. In two of my 13-week graduate courses, I include similar components. One course is called "Personal Change Paths." The other focuses on future possibilities for the professional helping enterprise and for each person in the class.

Nacke (1979) provided three-day workshops (developed by Thomas Brown) for Catholic Sisters to focus broadly on their ministry. Scott (1981) provided two-day workshops focusing on the human relations area for school board officials. In both types of workshops the desired outcome was a *plan* for further change. That is, people did not attend in order to learn *during* the workshop, but to set goals and plan strategies for achieving them. Life-planning workshops, women's consciousness-raising groups, and various peer self-help groups also help their members choose individual goals and strategies.

Individual help can be provided by phone or mail or in person, by professionals or trained lay volunteers or peers. One-to-one help with choosing and achieving change is already provided by some counselors and therapists, academic course advisors, thesis supervisors, mentors in nontraditional individualized education (Bradley, 1975), education information centers, educational brokering services (Heffernan, Macy, and Vickers, 1976), life- and career-planning counselors, leisure activities counselors, and staff and professional development officers. Perhaps the future will bring more counselors and centers devoted to fostering the entire range of intentional change, not just education or career or personality. I would like to see a center open 24 hours a day for quick questions by phone or in person, and smaller neighborhood centers open at convenient hours for longer appointments.

Many of these services can be financed in the same ways that other books, television programs, workshops, courses, and counseling are financed. Additional funding might be required for early-stage developmental costs, and for the overhead of a counseling and information center. Unfortunately, no one in government is responsible for the entire range of intentional change, and public funding for a comprehensive center may therefore be difficult. Centers related to jobs, education, reading, or recreation fit well in one government department or another, but comprehensive centers may not fit well in any one department.

It is important not only to develop and provide innovative help, but also to study its effects. What changes in the person's knowledge, self-image, self-direction, competence, attitude, and behavior occur as a result of the type of book, workshop, or counseling described in these first two directions? At this stage, it is important to remain open to the entire range of effects, as Nacke (1979) and Scott (1981) have done. We are not yet ready to eliminate all surprises by limiting our questions to a narrow range of effects. We can also try to discover what additional competence and help would be especially useful.

## Increase Information About Opportunities and Resources

It is not enough for the person to have clear goals and an appropriate choice of strategy. The person also needs full and accurate information about the effective resources, opportunities, methods, and paths available for this particular change. There is little point in having resources and methods available if the person is not aware of them, or lacks sufficient information to choose wisely. Many mechanisms already exist to provide this information, but they could be strengthened and expanded. In addition, innovative new ways of providing such information could be developed.

Information about available courses, workshops, seminars, human growth centers, conferences, and therapy groups is already provided by direct mail advertising, newspaper advertising, and catalogs. It is important to make this information complete and accurate in the first place, or to provide further details in a supplementary announcement that is available on request. In Toronto, a complete list of courses offered throughout the metropolitan area is available in all public libraries. By looking up yoga or French or human relations, for instance, any person can find the location, sponsor, time, and cost of every course in the city. Some cities have a central telephone number or information center that serves the same function. Toronto also has a 30-page monthly newsletter listing many meetings and events within the psychic and spiritual realms. Each institution could also have an open house at which people can get further information and meet the instructors and group leaders. Also, at special introductory sessions and the first regular session, the leader should spell out her or his objectives, methods, and expectations.

A model for full detailed information is provided by a 1979 brochure for a four-day life/work planning workshop called "What Color Is Your Parachute?" It spells out whom the workshop is for, quotes positive comments from previous participants but also states the number of persons (5 out of 225) who were negative, and provides details on meals and accommodations and commuting. Then a detailed section called "What is *Your* Learning Style, at Workshops?" describes nine dimensions or variables and locates this workshop on each dimension. To give the flavor, here is one of the nine paragraphs: "Some people learn best when material is presented in rapid order and style; while others learn best when the material is presented slowly and meticulously. You should attend this workshop only if you learn well in a slow-meticulous atmosphere. We go at a pace which enables everyone to keep up; this sometimes drives fast-learners crazy, in which case this is not the workshop for You, dear friend."

Various guides to television and radio programs are already widely available. However, I would like to see them include a weekly list of "Some particularly useful programs for your learning, change, and growth." Outstanding sports, entertainment, and dramatic programs could be noted in three other lists.

Information systems concerning books and periodical articles are well established. For almost any desired change, a person can find useful printed materials by consulting bibliographic tools and catalogs, annotated bibliographies, a librarian or bookstore clerk, or one of the newer computer information retrieval systems. Books are also brought to our attention by the book review section of newspapers and magazines, and by such tools as *Co-Evolution Quarterly.* Detailed information about available tapes, records, and videotapes is not as readily available.

For some changes, the person wants to find an expert or professional helper. Apart from asking friends, it is hard to get full and accurate information concerning this type of resource. I would like to see detailed directories, open houses or other semisocial occasions, or 20-minute videotapes available to those seeking an expert.

One excellent step in recent years is the learning network (Lewis, 1978; Lewis and Kinishi, 1977). A survey by Calvert and Draves (1978) found 42 of them in the United States. That report called them learning referral centers and stated that they are also known as learning networks, learning exchanges, and referral services. I originally thought they were limited to helping people find an instructor for such subjects as guitar, auto mechanics, and Spanish. The actual list of areas is far broader than I guessed and includes many areas of personal growth and lifestyle change. Robert Lewis, a cofounder of the first learning network (in Evanston), is now experimenting with a different model in Atlanta. Simple, yet extraordinarily effective at helping people find an expert or helper in practically any area, learning networks have enormous potential. They can be developed within a company, university, or professional association as well as in a city. I am often moved by their human drama stories of reducing loneliness, crossing generation and racial lines, and sparking large changes and learning efforts. Incidentally, the learning networks have discovered that most potential instructors do not view themselves as potential teachers. "Me! What would I teach? I'm just a car mechanic."

Sometimes the person seeks a partner or peer—someone who is interested in the same area or experiencing the same change— rather than an expert. Learning networks can assist with this function too. In addition, certain individuals in any community serve a natural linking function, spontaneously suggesting someone the person might want to talk to about a particular problem or interest. Exploratory efforts to support and encourage (not train!) these natural linking people could be useful.

How can a person get full and accurate information about available peer self-help groups and autonomous learning groups? Several cities now have directories of these groups, or a central telephone number or referral agency. Much more effort is needed, however, before most people will be aware of these groups and how to find them.

Our interviewees have also mentioned the need for complete, up-to-date, accurate information on various occupations, available jobs, and available apartments.

People also need plenty of accurate information concerning any methods or paths that are suited to their particular change. To some extent, such information is available. Such books as Matson (1977) and Lande (1976) describe a variety of paths and methods for personal change, a few books do the same for leisure activities, several books present self-insight and growth exercises, and many suggest paths for physical fitness and robust health. Even in these areas of change, and certainly in many others, people still have trouble obtaining enough accurate detailed information to choose the best option.

In the realm of intentional change, how long will it be until objective consumer information is readily available? At great expense, such information is compiled and disseminated concerning automobiles, stereos, retirement savings plans, mutual funds, insurance companies, drugs, even soap and diapers. It would be just as beneficial to have consumer ratings plus objective test results available for all the resources and opportunities in the area of intentional changes. What really are the outcomes of various spiritual and personal growth paths? Do the LSD techniques described by Grof (1975) produce the same effects as tedious Eastern religious techniques? Just how much change do people actually achieve through a self-guided approach? From which TV programs, newspapers, magazines, tours, and museums does one gain a reasonably accurate and complete picture of life on earth? How much do the previous customers say they gained from a particular therapist, instructor, leader, or program? What paths or methods of helpers are dangerous or harmful more often than others? How does the dropout rate or dissatisfaction rate vary from one path or agency to another?

## Reduce Undue Restrictions on Freedom of Choice

As a general principle, each man and woman who wants to change should usually be free to seek help from anyone who is willing to give that help, possibly in exchange for money, goods, or bartered services. Also, the man or woman should usually be free to choose *not* to seek help from anyone. Unfortunately, such freedom of choice is being eroded by some government actions, insurance plans, and professional associations. Those of us who are involved in the helping enterprise can make significant contributions toward reversing that erosion. Doing this will require a great deal from each of us: altruism, thoughtful exploration of the issues, and commitment to the entire range of intentional changes.

Let us look first at the issue of differential costs. Government funding and insurance reimbursement go largely to professional helpers and their institutions. Little or no money is available for the person doing the changing (even if that person is poor and needy) if he or she chooses to use nonprofessional helpers or other resources such as books. Funding goes to education, doctors and hospitals, therapists, and social workers rather than to the entire range of learning, health care, personal change, and problem-solving. The person does have a free choice if he or she can offer money or services to the helpers who require payment, but some choices are penalized by differential costs. In effect, government and insurance plans establish and support huge helping enterprises (at great financial cost to taxpayers and insurance plan contributors) without awareness of the narrowness of their funded portion. Perhaps 70 or 80% of all problem-solving, physical and mental health care, and learning could proceed without a professional, but some legislators and other policymakers ignore the person's natural process of choosing and guiding change. The general public, in turn, becomes less aware of alternative paths and helpers and comes to see the government-financed way as the only effective, normal, legitimate way.

Many companies reimburse employees for course tuition fees, but not for any costs of self-planned learning. Paid educational leave, a significant and growing trend in Europe and being studied in Canada, provides time and money for course-taking but not for learning in other ways. Students in colleges and universities receive financial benefits from government, but would lose them if they switched to learning on their own.

Next let us look at differential legitimacy. How would your boss react to your spending an afternoon in a university library reading in your field of expertise? Would the reaction be different if you spent that afternoon at a university-sponsored workshop in the same field?

To enter many professions and occupations, you must do your learning with the credentialed experts: learning in other ways and then demonstrating your competence in examination situations is simply not an option. It would be more effective if the person who wants to work at a particular occupation (electrician, nurse, lawyer, etc.) had a choice of several paths for achieving the desired competence. At least one of these paths might be preprogrammed or professionally controlled through tapes, programmed instruction, classes, or apprenticeship. At least one other path should be self-planned without a professional: it might consist of peer groups or individual paths, for instance. The person's choice of path should not be unduly restricted by requiring course attendance or academic credentials instead of demonstrated competence, nor by examinations biased in favor of one path.

Differential funding and legitimacy are not the only ways in which the person's range of choices is restricted. For certain types of changes, it is actually illegal to use certain helpers, or at least is illegal for them to provide help. Certain professional associations have persuaded governments to outlaw many potentially useful helpers. Physical health and law are the two most obvious examples: regardless of your expertise or effectiveness, you cannot practice medicine or law without a license. Illich (1978, p. 24) put it in his usual blunt way: "Unlike the hookers of old, the modern professional is not one who sells what others give for free, but rather one who decides what ought to be sold and must not be given for free." In fact, Illich (1978, p. 23) has gone even further and has claimed that professionals actually create the needs that they are then mandated to fill: "Educators and doctors and social workers today—as did priests and lawyers formerly—gain legal power to create the need that, by law, they alone will be allowed to serve."

Although Illich's criticism may be too severe, there is some evidence that professional licensing does not, in fact, serve the public interest. After reviewing the literature on professional licensing, psychologist S.J. Gross (1978b, p. 1015) concluded that "licensing arrangements do not seem to be providing the structure for effective solutions to the problems of delivering quality care in the health and helping services. Instead, the evidence overwhelmingly supports the conclusion that licensing maintains a structure that is in the self-interest of the service giver and in opposition to the public interest. Licensing actually results in the institutionalization of a lack of accountability to the public."

Many years earlier, economist Milton Friedman (1962) argued persuasively that there is no good reason to license any occupation, including medicine, because certification does as much good. Certification means that a governmental agency "may certify that an individual has certain skills but not prevent, in any way, the practice of any occupation using these skills by people who do not have such a certificate" (p. 144). One may have to pass an examination or meet certain other requirements before certification as a medical doctor, public accountant, architect, or psychologist, but anyone else would still be free to go into the business of accepting fees for helping people with their health, accounting, house design, or mental health. Under licensing, by contrast, one cannot practice the skills of the given occupation (at least, not for a fee) before passing the examination or meeting the other state requirements. "Anyone who does not have a license is not authorized to practice and is subject to a fine or jail sentence if he does engage in practice" (p. 145).

S.J. Gross (1978a) has proposed registered disclosure as an effective way to protect the consumer. People offering a service, such as counseling, to the public would be required by law to make available information about the nature, scope, philosophy, orientation, techniques, and requirements of that service. From this information, consumers would make decisions about the quality and appropriateness of such service. The information would be required to be complete and accurate, and governmental and judicial mechanisms would be extended to act on complaints about fraud.

Whether it is dance instruction or psychotherapy, physical fitness programs or self-help books, mind-control groups or religious groups, people should have ready access to reasonably complete and accurate information about the approach and its effectiveness. They should be free to make their own choice. They should also be free to quit or leave any time without intimidation, threats, heavy financial penalties, or other undue consequences. In my opinion, professional associations and governments should support these three conditions and should definitely not restrict the person's choice of groups, cults, helpers, books, and other resources and paths. If a government or professional association believes that one particular person or path is harmful, they can try to spread that message to the general public, and in some cases can prosecute under existing laws dealing with misleading advertising, high-pressure sales techniques, and violence or threats of violence.

My position is clear: freedom of choice is unduly restricted when one says, "If you want help with this particular problem or change, you must use these helpers and you cannot use or pay any other helpers." However, the person in that situation at least has the freedom of whether to proceed with the change, and whether to use any helpers at all.

An even greater restriction of choice can occur when one says, "You must get help from designated professionals with your particular problem or change, whether you want to proceed with it or not." Yet that is exactly what happens in certain situations. Most people accept the notion of mandatory professional intervention when someone has committed a violent crime. Most of us would agree with the need for an ambulance and medical attention without the person's consent if the person remains unconscious and seriously injured after an accident. Many people accept compulsory schooling for children (though the voices in opposition are becoming stronger). There is much less agreement on just how severe mental illness must be before the person is involuntarily committed to a mental hospital, though it is clear that the days of unnecessarily forcing some people into these hospitals have not yet ended.

Another example of forcing a person to enter a situation in which certain professional helpers try to change the person is provided by mandatory continuing education, which I prefer to call "compulsory sitting." This may be spreading. Members of several occupations must attend particular courses (or choose from several possibilities) for a certain number of hours, or suffer severe consequences. Instead of periodically testing competence or soliciting consumer evaluations, many states now require one *method* of learning (sitting in a course or workshop) for health care professionals, certified public accountants, lawyers, and others. The person must acquire a certain number of continuing education units in order to continue practicing her or his occupation: these units are granted for mere sitting, because there is no assessment of what people learn from these courses. Ignoring the astounding amount of highly effective and energetic self-planned learning that professionals engage in to improve their competence (McCatty, 1973), legislation forces them to learn from a professional instructor. Surely we should give credit for self-planned learning efforts instead of giving credit merely for sitting in certain rooms at certain times. Even better would be the development of adequate assessment procedures to test the person's competence periodically.

Lisman and Ohliger (1978) have charged that employees of industrial corporations are increasingly being pushed into training courses, parents of juvenile delinquents are sometimes ordered by the courts to obtain family guidance from social service agencies, some food stamp recipients are pressured to participate in nutrition programs, and some illiterates on welfare are ordered to enroll in adult basic education classes.

We have been discussing situations in which particular change methods or techniques (all involving professional helpers) are required. The opposite sort of restriction is to ban or outlaw certain methods, or to stamp them out in some other way. This is fairly rare, with one major exception. Because of highly inaccurate news stories and public beliefs, most national governments have banned intentional changes through LSD and other psychedelic drugs. Now, however, more balanced evidence is available concerning the benefits and risks of these drugs (Grinspoon and Bakalar, 1979; Grof, 1975). They are clearly of significant benefit for the intentional changes of some people, at least when used under appropriate supervision with known dosages of pure drugs. Surely the time has come to explore prudent ways of making psychedelic experiences legally available with appropriate screening or supervision.

Content, methods, and helpers vary enormously from one intentional change to another. How can one justify eliminating or requiring certain methods or helpers? In my opinion, undue restrictions on freedom of choice should be reduced. For each of us, the first step is to study the issues and literature carefully. Each of us will then be better able to develop a thoughtful position.

In addition to eliminating undue restrictions on freedom of choice, we can also foster intentional changes by offering a wide choice of opportunities and resources for people. We turn to that direction in the next section. We switch our focus now from avoiding the negative to enlarging the positive.

## Widen the Range of Opportunities and Resources

We can significantly facilitate intentional changes by ensuring a wide choice of options for the person's changes. Ideally people should be able to choose their changes from an excellent variety of possibilities, and then should be free to choose from several effective methods or resources. A pluralistic society is tolerant of a wide diversity of changes and paths as long as they do not unduly interfere with anyone else.

Mentally list the organizations that you know best, including the ones for which you work. Could their scope or mission or services be broadened to facilitate a wide range of individual changes? Are there fresh creative ways in which they could encourage and assist the entire range of intentional changes? Whenever you or your organization, department, or community group is facing a major decision, ask yourself a simple question: Which choice would increase the opportunities and resources for intentional changes?

Whenever given a choice, let's move toward greater variety of available jobs, lifestyles, marriage partners, homes, legal psychedelics, spiritual and religious paths, and personal growth methods. Let's encourage autonomous peer groups and self-help groups to form around common interests and needs. Let's encourage and finance a variety of methods of learning in the community and in a company, not just courses and workshops. Let's support self-directed learning or individual interaction with a learning consultant for disadvantaged persons and unemployed persons, instead of providing only classes and courses for them. Let's reduce the monopoly of the health establishment and permit people to seek health advice and treatment from a variety of practitioners. Let's be sure self-help books or periodicals are published to assist the entire range of intentional changes. Let's support public libraries and bookstores in small and rural communities as well as cities. A wide variety of cassette tapes, records, kits, films, and videotapes should also be widely available for borrowing or inexpensive purchase. Let's make available, and finance fairly, a range of counseling, therapy, and personal growth methods. Let's encourage special interest travel, tours, visits, and observations. Let's support innovative television programming, art galleries, public lectures and film showings, free universities, human growth groups, and empathy workshops.

Governments and institutions typically encourage and finance only the highly visible helping enterprise, the "overside," the professional and institutional activities, rather than the person's own natural process. Given the agency's supposed goal of fostering health, learning, or ability to cope with problems, fostering and financing the individual's process might be more effective and far less costly.

Professional associations and professional regulatory bodies should encourage fresh, innovative, emerging paths and forms of help for the person's changes. Only clear abuses should be dealt with when developing and enforcing regulations. During my many years as a member of the American Psychological Association, I have sometimes been amazed and chagrined at the enthusiastic efforts of some members to squelch an emerging variety of opportunities, techniques, and resources for change. The APA guidelines for "psychologists who conduct growth or encounter groups" insist on a screening interview or equivalent with every participant. If the group has a psychotherapeutic rather than an educational purpose, the guidelines also insist on "before and after consultation with any other therapist who may be professionally involved with the participant" (American Psychological Association, 1973, p. 933). I consider these restrictions barely acceptable, but I remember well my reaction to an earlier draft. I was so angry and baffled that it took me an hour to compose a very simple letter in response to that draft.

Then, at the annual APA meeting in 1978, I was astounded by the meeting of a small task force interested in controlling all self-help books and tapes produced by psychologists. In their well-intentioned zeal to eliminate dangerous abuses, they came dangerously close to controlling and repressing the fresh creative possibilities. No doubt many books give stupid or useless advice on marriage, divorce, searching for a job, nutrition, child-raising, religion, investments, breaking a habit, losing weight, and 101 other areas of life. Most people are aware of this situation and are reasonably competent at selecting suitable books or advice for their own needs. To me it does not make sense to try to screen and control the writing of the members of one professional association or even, as one person suggested, to issue an APA seal of approval for certain books and tapes. Surely it makes much better sense to help the lay public understand the uses and limits of self-help books, to publish contrary opinions when the public becomes interested in one opinion that seems wrong to other professionals, and to explore whether present laws are sufficient to control misleading claims and eliminate any resources that are actually dangerous.

Printed materials and television programs are useful in some intentional change projects. In recent years, these resources have become even more relevant to change by becoming more varied and focused. Magazines for special interests and activities have multiplied while some general mass-circulation magazines have folded. Multichannel cable TV with some community programming has widened the person's choice. Flexibility and access may improve even more dramatically over the next ten years. Libraries and information systems are being revolutionized by computer technology, making literature searches much quicker. Interactive television, perhaps combined with personal home computer capabilities, may bring greater access to information right into the home and office. The person may soon be able to use the home TV screen for fast searching and access to thousands or millions of published documents and practical facts. In experiments in several countries, the person can already see printed news on the home TV screen seconds after it is typed at the central news-gathering agency. Interactive television also provides a much wider range of TV programs and videotapes, including many self-education courses, with the possibility of individual choice of program or tape at any time. Youngblood (1977) sees a shift in the communications field from centralized one-way distribution of messages to two-way communication involving decentralized input as well as output. The mass audience is being replaced by special audiences or groups, and soon there will be "public access to information specified by the user and public access to communications channels controlled by the user" (p. 10).

## Improve Ongoing Support from Nonprofessionals

People who are intentionally changing receive a great deal of help and support from friends, relatives, and other nonprofessionals. We saw in chapter 4 that 68% of all the help came from this source. If such help were improved and more accessible, it could contribute even more to the success of intentional changes.

Educational and human services agencies might develop ways of strengthening and supporting nonprofessional help. Most people could improve the effectiveness of the help they give to their friends, family members, and coworkers. For instance, they might improve their empathy, thoughtfulness, genuineness, or caring in these helping interactions. They might become more knowledgeable about intentional changes, and thus offer better suggestions. Strengthening, supporting, and improving nonprofessional help is an enormously difficult enterprise, one in which we must be particularly careful to avoid doing more harm than good.

Professionals and organizations might also help people *find* suitable nonprofessional helpers or simply a partner in change. This could be done through a learning network or other means of listing or matching interested persons. We might also form and advertise (but not run) groups of persons going through similar changes, or simply a group of persons going through any sort of change or transition at all. Groups could also be formed to stimulate and support people who engage in a wide variety of self-planned learning projects (Tough, 1979, chap. 14).

Several studies have underlined the importance of fostering ongoing human support for those engaged in major efforts to change or learn.

Two decades ago, Cyril Houle interviewed people who were conspicuously engaged in learning. He concluded that "there is no doubt that most of the people studied felt that their learning activities were disparaged by their associates, and often this feeling was intense. [These people have] taken seriously the widely expressed belief that American society supports education, culture, or self-improvement wherever it is found—and they think they have discovered this belief to be untrue. . . . Many of the attitudes and values of American society are directly and specifically opposed to the idea of lifelong learning and . . . this opposition has a vehemence and spread of impact which is not apparent to those who do not feel it directly themselves. The enemy is not apathy, as many would like to believe, but outright opposition, and opposition from places where it counts most—from the family, associates, and friends who surround the person who feels an inclination toward learning" (1961, pp. 44-46).

Stimulated by Houle's research, I studied the person's difficulties and help during major learning efforts. Several interviewees would have liked encouragement and support in dealing with their doubts about their progress and competence, and others wanted the stimulation and companionship of others engaged in the same change or learning (Tough, 1967, pp. 66 and 70).

Vida Stanius and I distributed an early version of *Expand Your Life* (Tough, 1980) to 100 interested persons, and interviewed many of them about their experiences with that tool. One of our questions asked, "What other tools or help would have been useful?" Many of the responses expressed the need for a person who could listen, understand, help clarify the change, or encourage the interviewee not to abandon the change.

McGinnis interviewed 40 persons regarding their changes over a five-year period. He then stated, "I was struck by the relatively large number of [interviewees] who felt the lack of some human support during their process of change. They were referring generally to an individual who could understand their situation but was not a 'professional helper.' Perhaps adult educators could organize informational centers which would attempt to put people who needed some support during their process of change in touch with other members of the community who had experienced a similar change or were in the midst of such a change" (1975, p. 201).

The Society for the Advancement of Continuing Education for Ministry (1978) studied several group programs designed to help clergy plan their directions and strategies for personal and professional change. Many respondents emphasized the importance of continuing afterward to meet with one or more colleagues for support, discipline, and integration.

In the interviews conducted specifically for this book, the need for developing better support stood out clearly. In one question (6A in the Appendix) we asked for the one most difficult part of the person's total experience in choosing, planning, and achieving the change. One-quarter of the respondents gave replies indicating that they would have gained from a supportive group or partner. Some of them needed someone to help them actually continue the new behavior: the behavior itself was easy enough, but it was hard to remember to do it or to discipline oneself. Others needed someone to bolster their confidence in their ability to achieve the change. Some would have benefited from support to help overcome the sense of loss at what had to be given up as part of the change.

Later in the interview (question 9E) we asked what additional help "in the form of a particularly helpful or encouraging person, an expert, a group, or a professional" would have been beneficial. The most common response was a friend or other person with whom to talk over the change. A smaller number of interviewees said they would have benefited from more support or less blocking from a particular family member.

## Improve the Effectiveness of Professional Helpers

A final significant direction for action is to increase the effectiveness of professional and paraprofessional helpers. Improving their effectiveness would greatly benefit the change efforts of their clients, students, and patients.

Each helper can choose from a variety of paths for improvement. For instance, a helper can read about intentional changes, read about becoming an effective and innovative helper, discuss problems and methods with colleagues, attend a workshop or professional association meeting, observe a colleague in action, invite that colleague to return the visit and offer suggestions, try to listen better to each client, attend an empathy-training or personal-growth group, try to be more loving or spontaneous or authentic, study his or her own change efforts. In order to choose directions in which to improve, a helper can also seek constructive feedback by observing the client's or student's reactions, by reflection after a helping session, by taping one session and listening to the tape a few weeks later, or by directly asking the clients or students to make suggestions individually, in a small group, or in writing.

I also urge all helpers to interview five of the people they help. This requires simply asking five people individually or in a group to describe their recent change efforts, using some of the questions in the Appendix. It is important to give each person an hour or two to reply at leisure and in some depth. Five or ten hours spent at this listening can transform a helper. He or she will see that the person's own ongoing efforts to change are common, normal, and effective. Many people are capable, powerful, and successful much of the time, and are willing to change rather than unduly resistant or static. Through interviews, a helper may also see how the particular sorts of changes that he or she facilitates are embedded within the person's total range of intentional changes.

I first became aware of the powerful impact of interviews a few years ago in my graduate course on self-guided learning and change. I required each student to interview five persons. The most dramatic change occurred in a literacy teacher who had himself experienced poverty and who was clearly sensitive to illiterate and working-class persons. Through interviews with five of his students, however, he gained much greater appreciation for the life of illiterate and working-class people, and realized deeply that they were adequate, fully functioning persons with full lives rather than deficient. He summarized his experience by saying quietly, "Those five interviews raised my consciousness more than I thought anything could."

As the helper becomes more familiar with the natural ongoing process of intentional changes and with their effectiveness, he or she may try harder to build on that process or to fit into it. Instead of imposing goals on the person, the effective helper tries to help each particular individual clarify and choose the highest-priority goals, no matter how specific or narrow these are. Instead of imposing his or her favorite methods, the effective helper tries to fit flexibly into each particular person's process and preferred style. Such a helper may also suggest a variety of methods, exercises, and books for the person to consider exploring after a helping session. The effective helper neither overcontrols nor undercontrols the choice of goals and strategy. Many professional helpers and fields are shifting from overcontrol to shared responsibility. Achieving the optimum amount of professional control is so important that it deserves a separate chapter.

# Chapter 6

# An Optimum Amount of Professional Control

We turn now to a particularly important implication from our data. We saw in earlier chapters that the typical adult successfully chooses and achieves beneficial changes without much help. The person's natural process of intentional change is remarkably effective. Those of us who are professional helpers might be able to build on that natural process. Instead of having too much or too little control, we can shift toward effectively sharing with the person the responsibility for choosing, planning, and implementing changes. The more I learn about intentional changes, the more convinced I become that shifting to the optimum amount of control is a particularly urgent and important implication, a particularly promising direction for improving our contribution to intentional changes.

In this chapter we will focus on one dimension of the interaction that occurs between the changing person and a significant helper. The latter might be a professional helper, such as a counselor, instructor, doctor, therapist, librarian, or social worker. It might be a trained paraprofessional helper in a community agency, crisis center, school, or church. Much of this chapter will also apply to a parent serving as a helper with his or her children, although only one section is written with that purpose in mind.

In any given helping relationship, does the professional helper have an appropriate amount of control, or too much, or too little? That is our central dimension and question in this chapter. Helpers commonly overcontrol, but occasionally a helper will err in the opposite direction.

Power and control is a significant recurring theme in various fields and professions. Carl Rogers devoted an entire book to examining "power and control in relationships between people" (1977, p. xii) in field after field: education, politics, marriage, and family. A book edited by Fischer and Brodsky (1978) examined the amount of professional control in various human service fields, such as special education, psychological assessment, industrial consulting, classroom teaching, psychiatry, prison management, psychotherapy, medical treatment, maintaining pupil records, and psychological experimentation. A major review of teaching methods research stated that a primary dimension in the vast majority of these studies is the degree to which the teacher exercises control over the behavior of the students (Wallen and Travers, 1963, p. 470).

How much control does the helper have? We can imagine a situation in which he or she has 100% of the control and authority, and the changing person has virtually no power at all. This is represented by the extreme left-hand end of the continuum in figure 1. At the opposite extreme, the person could retain full control, turning none of it over to the helper. This situation, 100% freedom and autonomy, is represented by the right-hand end of the continuum.

This is a useful dimension because it enables us to compare various helping and teaching situations on a crucially important variable. You might find it fascinating to mark on the continuum

| 0 | 100% |
|---|---|
| The person has zero control because the helper has complete control. | The person retains 100% of the control. |

**Figure 1.** Who Controls the Choice of the Change, the Strategy Decisions, and the Implementation Activities?

various helping relationships and situations that you have experienced. The fact that it is a continuum also avoids black-and-white thinking: instead of assuming a situation as either helper-controlled or completely free, we realize it can be somewhere in between.

## Optimum Range of Control

The continuum is particularly useful in enabling us to compare the actual amount of control with the optimum amount. For any given helper, person, and intended change, there will be an optimum or ideal range on the continuum. In one set of circumstances the person's ideal range of control might be 60–80%, in another situation, 40–60%, and quite different in a third situation. If the helper and the changing person stay within this range, the intended change (and the person's future willingness and ability to choose and guide a change) will be facilitated more than if they move higher or lower on the continuum.

I believe that each of us, when serving as a helper or parent, should avoid overcontrol and undercontrol. We should aim to keep inside the optimum range for this particular person and situation. If in doubt, we should lean toward too little control rather than too much.

We have already seen, in earlier chapters, that most persons have a remarkably rich and successful natural process for choosing, planning, and implementing their changes. They largely handle these tasks on their own, with some help from friends and family. I believe we should usually try to fit into that natural process in a light-handed manner. We can provide helpful information, offer suggestions and our reasons for them, point out the options and their costs and benefits. Note that this sort of help does not take away from the person any of the responsibility for making the major decisions. For me, this makes better sense than intruding in a heavy-handed manner, oblivious to the person's own natural process, being far more controlling and directing and "in charge" than necessary.

As professional helpers, most of us sometimes ignore, distort, or interfere with the person's natural ongoing process of choosing, planning, and implementing changes. Instead of treasuring that process, and fostering and facilitating it, we sometimes take over complete control of the process. Instead of fitting into the person's natural process, we force the person to fit into our process. My guess is that professional and paraprofessional helpers fairly often control more than the optimum range in figure 1; they control more than is necessary for the person to change effectively. In short, we would often be more helpful if we controlled less. We have seen how effective and successful the person's natural process can be, but all too rarely do we use that powerful personal process as a foundation on which to base our help.

My initial professional training was as a high school teacher of mathematics and English. I was successfully trained to do what classroom teachers do. To earn some income during my teacher training, I tutored a girl in grade ten mathematics. I was surprised to discover that the way I had learned to teach did not fit into her needs and process at all. To be effective with her, I had to behave quite differently from the way I operated as a classroom instructor. I had to sense her natural ongoing learning process in geometry, and then fit into "where she was at."

Not until ten years later did I come across some research that confirmed my experience. Combs (1969) found, in a wide range of helping situations, that the helper's spontaneous responses in the immediate situation (along with positive perceptions of self and others) are far more important for effecting change than are the helper's training, techniques, and theoretical background.

Lyon (1974) has urged that we treat our students, employees, and children the way we treat sunsets "instead of trying to reform them or change them with our 'superior knowledge' of how they ought to be" (p. 505). "When you look at a sunset no one says, 'It needs a little more orange in the cloud cover, a little more pink on the right hand side.' You allow it to become. That's one of the joys of sunsets—they're all unique. You allow them to be just what they are" (p. 505).

Several writers have decried or documented our tendency toward professional overcontrol. Some of them may be rather extreme, but they have performed a useful service in drawing our attention to the control dimension. In five hospitals, Roth (1972) studied institutional control over the behavior of the clientele. Farber (1970) made some biting comments about educational institutions: "Students are niggers. When you get that straight, our schools begin to make sense. . . . The faculty and administrators decide what courses will be offered; the students get to choose their own Homecoming Queen" (pp. 90–91). In a bitter attack on the mental health profession, medicine, and social work, Schrag (1978) suggested that professional helpers do not recognize the private and the ineffable (which might include the person's natural process of change). They want to control, and cannot tolerate uncertainty and the unpredictable. Illich has declared, "I propose to call the mid-twentieth century the Age of Disabling Professions" (1978, p. 16). Turning specifically to learning and education, he decries "the world-wide discrimination against the autodidact" (p. 16). Professional helpers communicate to the client, "You are deficient; you are the problem," according to McKnight (1977, p. 83). "As *you* are the problem, the assumption is that *I,* the professionalized servicer, *am the answer. You* are not the answer. *Your peers* are not the answer." McKnight also stated that professionals are increasingly claiming the power to decide whether their help is effective. "The client is viewed as a deficient person, unable to know whether he has been helped" (p. 87).

Sometimes professionals keep the person in the dark about their diagnosis, treatment, progress, and likely outcomes. "Don't question; don't try to understand; don't ask me to share my knowledge and expertise with you" is sometimes the message. As a result, the person cannot take an active informed part in the decision-making, and does not gain a larger repertoire of skills or techniques for choosing and achieving future changes. By contrast, in a very inspiring and courageous address that I recall vividly, George A. Miller (1969) urged professionals to "give psychology away" to make psychological knowledge and principles readily available to anyone who can use them beneficially.

So far we have been talking about the optimum amount of professional control in a face-to-face situation, either one-to-one or in a group. Books, too, vary in the extent to which the author tries to control the directions and strategies for change. Some self-help books tell the person exactly what change to strive for, and provide a complete step-by-step procedure for achieving that change. At the opposite end of the continuum, some books help the person choose both the direction and the strategy for change. Somewhere in the middle, Coates and Thoresen (1977) suggest and explain various steps and techniques, but also encourage readers to study their own patterns and develop their own combination of strategies.

## The Issue of Control for Three Tasks

In chapter 4, we distinguished three broad tasks that are required for intentional change: choosing the desired change, planning the strategy, and taking the actual steps for achieving the change. Let us now briefly examine the issue of control for each of these tasks in turn.

With the first task, choosing the change goal, it is particularly important for each of us to struggle against our natural urge to control others. People should be free to choose their own changes, without undue pressure. Each of us, however, sometimes tries to impose our own goals on the other person, either overtly or without the person's awareness and consent. This occurs partly because each of us, as a professional, is devoted to our own area of professional competence or subject matter, rather than to helping people with their total range of potential changes. Sometimes, though, we become too similar to the manufacturers and advertisers whose goal is to sell whatever they have, through convincing people that they need it.

It is natural for each of us to wish that we could somehow make people change in certain ways. If we could just somehow get people to avoid driving after drinking, to refrain from smoking at meetings, to conserve energy, to protest first-strike nuclear weapons, or to be kinder to their children, the world would be a better place. How can we encourage people to change in ways that are beneficial to others? One possibility is to inform the general public about the need for such changes. Through advertising, speeches, demonstrations, organizations, workshops, setting an example, letters to the editor, and other printed materials we can encourage changes that are especially beneficial for society. Some changes, such as avoiding driving after drinking alcohol, are so important that they must be required by law. In my opinion, though, we should hesitate to legislate or compel a change, or subtly coerce or persuade the person to "choose" it, unless we are certain it is essential for the welfare of all.

With the second task, deciding the strategy for change, we professionals are particularly likely to overcontrol. We are so well trained and confident in certain strategies that we become blind to other possibilities. We assume that the techniques of our particular specialty are just what everyone needs.

We turn now to the third task, actually taking the steps that will produce the change. It is quite often appropriate for the person to turn over control and responsibility for this task to a professional helper. In these cases the helper teaches, conducts therapy sessions, reinforces the desired changes, performs surgery, or whatever. Even with this task, however, the professional helper often takes over too much of the control. Once people have performed the first two tasks successfully, they are often quite capable of performing the third task with little or no professional help.

## Some Causes of Overcontrol

As I listen to person after person describe their successful self-guided changes, I wonder why professional helpers sometimes try to overcontrol. Why don't they, with a light touch, simply fit into the person's ongoing natural process of change? Why don't they always give the optimum amount of advice and help instead of sometimes taking over more control than is effective? Why do I and other instructors feel an urge to control what and how our students learn? Why do I and other parents want to tell our kids what to do, how to live, when to go to sleep, and who their friends should be? Why do some husbands have such difficulty in cheerfully leaving their wives free to choose their own activities, interests, friends, work, and life directions? Why are we reluctant to actively encourage our children, students, clients, or patients to be free, to make their own choices without being influenced by our preferences?

In short, what are some of the forces or causes of our human urge to overcontrol others? The various answers to this question can be grouped into six clusters.

1. The professional (and the paraprofessional and the parent) may simply have a false belief or norm: "In the occupation or role I'm in, the appropriate behavior is to be in control of the process and its outcomes. That's simply what we (therapists, teachers, doctors, etc.) do now and have always done. If I sat back and let the person flounder with decisions and methods, I'd obviously be very lazy and not living up to my responsibilities and not earning my money. Besides, it wouldn't work well." Professional training, subtle pressure from colleagues, or the need for license renewal may contribute to this belief or norm. Also, some professional helpers habitually use a set method or approach or sequence, and have simply never thought of the possibility of letting the person choose some other approach.

2. Do you have strong views on what should, and should not, be learned by children in schools? Most of us become upset occasionally when we hear of some change in the curriculum or its emphasis. We *care* whether sex education, human relations, religion, local history, explicit novels, peace, or team sports are included in the curriculum. Perhaps this reaction points to a common human ten-

dency. We strongly want certain sorts of people to learn certain things or change in some definite way. We have certain values, certain beliefs about what is right or important or worthy. No wonder we sometimes find ourselves pushing our children, clients, or patients toward certain specific changes and paths.

3. Deep-seated emotional needs may contribute to high control. As a helper, we may feel happy, strong, or adequate when in control of someone else's change, and may fear the consequences of losing that control. One insightful psychotherapist said to me, after reading the first draft of this section, "I am aware that, for me, control in an interpersonal situation is a way to overcome my fears and insecurities." Being "one up" may feel good: being on a pedestal and looked up to by others may enhance one's self-esteem (Tough, 1979, chap. 14). Gibb (1978, p. 109) has pointed out the "needs of the leader to feel special." Wanting to feel useful and important, to be a rescuer, to have an impact on the world are fairly common human wants. Perhaps the desire to influence one's client in significant ways is little different from the desire to build dams and bridges, to become a corporation president, or to direct a large research and development project.

It is important to note that most overcontrol occurs for very human and understandable reasons, not from greed, malice, or a professional conspiracy. In fact, most professionals are probably simply unaware of their overcontrol and its causes.

4. Sometimes a helper does not treasure autonomy and self-direction in other persons. The helper may be unaware of the amazing diversity in people and their successful directions and paths. In short, the helper may not trust the effectiveness and responsibility of the person choosing and guiding the changes, and may assume that a particular client will change much more effectively with firm guidance from the professional. If the helper does not treasure diversity, autonomy, and self-direction among colleagues and clients, then it will not seem sensible to foster individual choice of directions and paths. Perhaps only 1% of the population reaches a high integrated level of ego development that involves the cherishing of individuality. Perhaps not till the level just below that, called the autonomous stage, does one recognize and respect the other person's needs for autonomy (Loevinger, Wessler, and Redmore, 1970, pp. 6, 10). Only at these two high levels is there "a feeling for the complexity and multifaceted char-

acter of real people and of real situations. There is a deepened respect for other people and their need to find their own way and even make their own mistakes. Crucial instances are, of course, one's own children and one's own parents."

5. In a crisis or a particularly difficult situation, the helper may revert to being authoritarian, traditional, heavy-handed, and controlling. This experience has been reported to me by several instructors who were successfully reducing their control in normal nonstressful situations.

6. Some particularly important and fascinating causes of overcontrol lie within the person being helped. This cluster of causes is a particularly high-priority area for further research. The typical person strongly expects the doctor, teacher, or therapist to take over control of the process. Especially if the person is investing much time and money, he or she may expect some sort of dramatic action by the helper. Students, patients, and clients can become very upset and anxious, even angry and hostile, if the professional fails to fit the expected role, especially if responsibility and effort are shifted to the student or client. Students have succeeded for years at the game of schooling and do not want the rules suddenly changed. We become our own enemies or oppressors: we do it to ourselves, resisting efforts by the instructor or others to increase our responsibility and control. We feel frightened by the first taste of freedom granted by a professional helper, and we fight to retain the status quo.

One of my favorite true stories was told to me by a thoughtful acquaintance called Terry. One day Terry was listening to a friend of his who is a medical doctor. She was complaining about the behavior of her patients: they refused to accept responsibility for their own health and resisted her efforts toward a partnership approach instead of complete doctor control. "Why can't they get up off their knees?" she pleaded. Terry then gently asked her how she behaved when she went to her own doctor. After a stunned moment she swore and said, "You're right. I put him on a pedestal and get down on my knees!"

## Shifting from Overcontrol to Shared Responsibility

We have seen that professional helpers sometimes overcontrol for various reasons. Instead of fitting into the person's effective natural process, they sometimes try to impose their own process and goals. The effectiveness of their help is reduced because they sometimes operate to the left of the optimum range in figure 1.

Many helpers, though, especially during the past few years, have been shifting their position in figure 1. By reducing their own control and letting the person retain plenty of control, they are moving into the optimum range on the continuum. They maximize their usefulness by avoiding the two extremes of overcontrol and undercontrol.

In various fields and professions, these helpers are moving toward shared responsibility with the person. They collaborate. Together they set goals and choose strategies. The professional shares his or her knowledge and expertise with the person, and enthusiastically fits into the person's needs and ongoing natural process. Neither person is on a pedestal nor one down. The helper treasures the person's competence at choosing and guiding changes and the person's success with previous changes. The person's self-image is enhanced. The person feels free, empowered, hopeful, able. His or her change proceeds more effectively and with high energy and enthusiasm. The person becomes more willing and able to take on ever greater responsibility with the next change effort.

There is a delightful paradox here. By striving and controlling less, the professional is actually more helpful. Shared responsibility works better than helper overcontrol. Once this situation is experienced (beyond the initial period of fear and resistance that sometimes occurs), both persons become enthusiastic. After seeing my students learning and changing effectively and enthusiastically with shared responsibility, for instance, I could not return to the overcontrolling way in which I used to teach.

Throughout this chapter it is essential to avoid black-and-white thinking. I am not proposing that the ideal position on the continuum is the extreme right-hand end ("the person retains 100% of the control"). Nor do professional literature and training urge helpers to operate at the other extreme ("the person has zero control because the helper has complete control"). What is happening now is simply a shift along the continuum to a more effective point, to an optimum range, but not to an extreme position. We are learning to reconcile the opposites, to find an effective middle position that will attract people who were formerly at one extreme or the other. I am indebted to Claudio Naranjo for pointing out (in a 1975 workshop) the important need for reconciling the opposites, for finding a way of bringing together people and positions at extremes such as hedonism and social action, or discipline and permissiveness. I hope the people who are usually near one end of the continuum in figure 1 will be able to listen to helpers at other positions and to see the effectiveness of a flexible position somewhere between the opposite poles.

In a moment we will turn to various specific fields such as health, counseling and psychotherapy, personal growth, social work, adult learning, education (higher, elementary, and secondary), library practice, religion, parenting, and personal liberation movements. In each field we will examine some of the recent efforts to move from high professional control to shared responsibility. First, though, let us look at some writing that is too broad to fit into just one field.

For me, the quotation that best captures the recent trend was written by Spragg (1978). She captures the spirit and the breadth of "this yet-to-be-named movement" in the following words: "People are trying to take charge of their own personal lives; they are taking back power and control. People are learning about their physical and spiritual well-being and taking back some of the power they have given over to the medical profession. Learners are deciding what and how they will learn instead of leaving that up to the educational institutions. People are taking assertiveness training and doing life planning so they can more effectively take charge of their present and future modes of living. And people are getting together in groups and taking back, in bits and pieces, the power that over the course of the 20th C. they had relinquished to big government and giant corporations and we hear talk of neighborhood government, appropriate technology and local self-reliance." Incidentally, Susan Spragg is an active young woman who not only writes about these matters, but also works on related action projects. She was involved in a Denver Free University experiment to foster "self-directed living," and is now writing a manual on self-directed learning.

The opening paragraph of *The Next Whole Earth Catalog* (Brand, 1980, p. 2) includes these words: "A realm of intimate, personal power is developing—the power of individuals to conduct their own education, find their own inspiration, shape their own environment, and share the adventure with whoever is interested." A decade earlier, Maslow (1969, p. 732) pointed out the need to develop "the self-evolving person, the responsible-for-himself-and-his-own-evolution person."

Summarizing several studies, Combs (1969) found remarkable similarities among the most effective helpers regardless of whether they were counselors, teachers, priests, or professors. The most effective helpers "are characterized by a generally positive view of their subjects and a belief in the capacity of the human organism to save itself. It makes a great deal of difference whether helpers perceive their clients as able or unable. If a counselor, teacher, or priest does not regard his clients as able he can hardly permit them, let them, or trust them to act on their own; to do so would be a violation of responsibility" (p. 72). Effective helpers tended to see their clients as dependable and worthy as well as able (p. 73). They also saw their tasks more as freeing than controlling (p. 74).

In his middle seventies, Carl Rogers wrote a fresh comprehensive book on personal power (1977), subtitled on the dust jacket *Inner Strength and Its Revolutionary Impact*. In assessing that book, biographer Kirschenbaum (1979, p. 431) points out its significance in this way: "Whether or not those forces in civilization which aim to give each person dignity, respect and control over his or her life are ultimately triumphant, Rogers will have taken a stand and played a part in the outcome."

In *Tools for Conviviality* (1973, p. xxiv), Illich distinguished whether tools restrict or enhance the person's control and power. "Scientific discoveries can be used in two opposite ways. The first leads to specialization of functions, institutionalization of values, and centralization of power—and turns people into the accessories of bureaucracies or machines. The second enlarges the range of each person's competence, control, and initiative, limited only by other individuals' claims to an equal range of power and freedom."

A comprehensive book on client participation in human services (Fischer and Brodsky, 1978) is subtitled *The Prometheus Principle*. That principle is stated thus: "Knowledge, power, and responsibility should be shared by all parties engaged in offering human services with those receiving such services" (p. ix). More precisely, the principle asserts that "if a citizen is to make optimal use of the human services professions, he must be enfranchised to participate actively both in the gathering and evaluation of information, and then in subsequent decision making and reckoning" (p. vii).

During the past few years, peer self-help groups or mutual aid groups have received much attention from social scientists (see, for example, Lieberman and others, 1979). According to our data in chapter 4, however, people receive even more nonprofessional help in individual one-to-one situations.

A particularly comprehensive and useful book about peer self-help groups has been written by Gartner and Riessman (1977). These groups have been developing rapidly in the fields of mental health, health, social work, and perhaps education. The authors point out that "one of the most significant characteristics of mutual aid groups is the fact that they are *empowering* and thus potentially dealienating. They enable their members to feel and use their own strengths and their own power and to have control over their own lives. This empowering dimension is extremely important for health and mental health" (p. 99). Gartner and Riessman also stated (p. 13) that human services should be centered on the client instead of the professional, and should recognize "the major extent to which the consumer serves himself or herself." On the same page they call for "a fundamental restructuring of the basic nature of the human services. The consumer, not the professional, should stand at the center. . . . Everett Hughes . . . once defined a 'quack' as one who satisfies his clients, but not his peers—a client-centered practice would label as a quack one who satisfies his or her professional peers, but not his or her clients!"

We turn now to several particular fields. In each one I will point out a few examples of recent and current efforts to shift from high professional control to shared responsibility and collaboration. Over the next few years, I hope these fields will strive to create and spread additional practices and techniques that incorporate this important shift.

## Physical Health

In several movements within the health field, control and responsibility are being shifted from doctors, nurses, and hospitals to the patient. Most of these movements are still small compared to the total field of health care, but are flourishing and rapidly expanding.

1. Information and education for patients is one of these movements. Williamson and Danaher (1978) document the highly active process that people undertake in seeking information and help after noting symptoms. Increasingly detailed and sophisticated books on health care are being published for the intelligent lay-public. To provide access to medical information and tools, physician Tom Ferguson began *Medical Self-Care* Magazine in 1976. Classes for adults are becoming widespread. Here are the results found by

physician Keith Sehnert, a pioneer in the recent spread of courses for activated patients. "Many of my patients already are their own doctors—sometimes. They've learned to handle minor illnesses and emergencies without help, and major ones without panic. They have 'black bags' of their own, with everything from stethoscope to sphygmomanometer in them. They examine their youngsters' ears with otoscopes when they complain of earaches. They check husbands' and wives' heartbeats and neighbors' blood pressures. . . . They are members of that brand-new breed, the Activated Patient—a kind of hearty hybrid who is three-quarters patient and one-quarter physician. They've learned to speak the doctor's own language, and ask him questions rather than passively sit, honor and obey. . . . They are playing an important and needed role in a health partnership with their doctors" (Sehnert, 1975, p. 3).

2. Peer self-help groups are available for virtually every major health problem. In these groups, peers are the source of information and advice, and each member not only receives help but also helps others. Gartner and Riessman (1977, pp. 75–77) divide these mutual help health organizations into four categories.

- Rehabilitative groups help and encourage patients to adjust to their new condition after mastectomy, ostomy, heart attack or stroke, kidney transplant, or cancer.
- Behavior change groups help their members reduce weight, smoking, alcohol, or other drug abuse.
- Primary care groups are useful where no cure is available, but where chronic care is important. Examples are emphysema, arthritis, and diabetes.
- A smaller number of self-help groups are concerned with prevention and with case finding.

3. A few doctors and clinics are experimenting with having patients (or the parents of very young patients) keep their own medical records, or at least have access to them. This is a move away from the doctor exclusively owning all the knowledge and the expertise.

4. Certain techniques for actively controlling and healing one's own body are rapidly spreading. Of course, people have always been able to control and heal certain conditions, but the range of techniques is expanding. They include biofeedback, relaxation exercises, and imaging.

5. The women's movement has provided health education and information for many women, and has founded several women-run clinics and health centers. The movement has challenged the overall structure of health care as it affects women, particularly the influence exerted by male doctors.

6. Doctors are moving away from center stage during childbirth and are turning that central position over to the mother (natural childbirth) and father (now in the delivery room—a dramatic change since 14 years ago when I was not allowed in). More recently, thanks to the work of French physician Frederick Leboyer, the infant is entitled to center stage. The medical establishment's tendency toward drugs, surgery, and high technology during childbirth is still startlingly strong, though. In Metropolitan Toronto, a task force proposed a central intensive care unit for all high-risk births and "a computerized central registry in which every local pregnant woman would be risk-screened": it rejected a much less expensive plan combining education, nutrition, genetic counseling, midwives, and research (Worthington and Scanlon, 1979).

7. Holistic health centers and practitioners are becoming more widespread. Their approach focuses on emotional and spiritual well-being along with physical health. It also places major responsibility on the person to be at least as active as the professional in prevention and healing.

8. Care of dying patients is being discussed and transformed largely as the result of the pioneering efforts of physician Elisabeth Kubler-Ross. She raised the consciousness of many of us regarding dying persons: they are full-fledged persons with insight, a desire for authentic personal dialogue, and often a distaste for an impersonal high-technology environment. More dying patients, especially children and parents of young children, are being cared for in their natural home environment in the final stages. Hospices, too, are creating a more natural homelike environment in which the patient feels more fully human and significant than in some hospital situations. In some U.S. states, patients with incurable illnesses may now direct their physician to withhold or withdraw life-sustaining equipment without fear of legal liability.

9. Some hospitals and patients' groups have developed lists of patients' rights. A few hospitals give their bill of rights to all patients on admission.

## Psychotherapy, Counseling, and Personal Growth

Carl Rogers begins his book on personal power (1977, p. 3) with the following story:

> Three years ago I was first asked about the politics of the client-centered approach to psychotherapy. I replied that there was no politics in client-centered therapy, an answer which was greeted with a loud guffaw. When I asked my questioner to explain, he replied, "I spent three years of graduate school learning to be an expert in clinical psychology. I learned to make accurate diagnostic judgments. I learned the various techniques of altering the subject's attitudes and behavior. I learned subtle modes of manipulation, under the labels of interpretation and guidance. Then I began to read your material, which upset everything I had learned. You were saying that the power rests not in my mind but in his organism. You completely reversed the relationship of power and control which had been built up in me over three years. And then you say there is no politics in the client-centered approach!"

In psychotherapy, counseling, and personal growth, most practitioners are trying or hoping to facilitate certain changes in the person, and most clients are intentionally seeking certain changes. In order to facilitate change more effectively, some professional helpers are trying to shift their stance from professional overcontrol to shared responsibility.

1. Both Carl Rogers and Arthur Combs (Combs, Avila, and Purkey, 1978) have been important in spreading a new view of the therapist. The key characteristics of effective helpers are their spontaneity, empathy, acceptance, respect, caring, self-concept, beliefs, and authenticity, not just their professional knowledge and techniques. They perceive and treat their clients as responsible, powerful, and competent. "The therapist becomes the 'midwife' of change, not its originator. . . . The locus of evaluation, of decision, rests clearly in the client's hands" (Rogers, 1977, p. 15). Richard Farson (1978, p. 9) believes that Rogers "invented a technique to eliminate technique." To be more specific, what happens is that "the therapist enters without benefit of technique, meeting the client person to person, not in control, vulnerable to whatever happens."

2. Within the field of behavior modification, some practitioners are moving toward self-managed change (Kazdin, 1978; Coates and Thoresen, 1979). Clients play a significant role in setting the targets for change, in choosing and modifying a set of strategies, in recording certain information about their own behavior, and in implementing these strategies. Kazdin also devotes half a chapter to certain techniques of cognitive behavior modification, such as rational-emotive therapy and self-instruction training.

3. Cocounseling, too, leaves the control of the process largely in the hands of the person with the problem. Even more important, the whole notion of one person being "one up" and the other being "one down" vanishes because the two people take turns being counselor and client. Two women I know, for example, charge each other $100 an hour for counseling. No money has yet changed hands because they have each received the same number of hours. One widespread form of organized cocounseling is Re-evaluation Counseling, founded by Harvey Jackins. Another leader in cocounseling, especially in Britain, is John Heron. He has provided an excellent foundation for understanding the process in his monograph on catharsis (1977).

4. W.R. Miller (1978) reported encouraging results with many problem drinkers who were given a self-help manual in lieu of group or individual therapy sessions.

5. Especially interested in how mental health professionals can intervene in the person's social network, Sarason (1977, p. 165) has listed six intervention strategies:

> First, family therapists have expanded their work into the social network of schizophrenics. Second, social scientists have worked with large peer groups of urban "dropouts" in an attempt to reach these youth effectively. Third, an institutional psychotherapist has tried to change a resident's network that he conceptualizes as a support for deviant or prosocial behavior. Fourth, community mental health practitioners have moved beyond the environments of families and schools to include all the essential people in a client's network to work towards a solution of the problems. Fifth, mental health people have intervened in networks of people in a crisis situation. Sixth, community mental

health professionals have intervened in naturally occurring day-care networks to improve their scope and functioning.

6. The President's Commission on Mental Health, too, focused attention on the importance of strengthening natural networks. It studied the possibility of "a major new Federal initiative in community mental health to . . . recognize and strengthen the natural networks to which people belong and on which they depend— families, kin, kith, friendship, and neighborhood social networks; work relationships, religious denominations and congregations; and self-help groups and other voluntary associations based on principles of intimacy and mutual aid" (Task Panel on Community Support Systems, 1978, p. 154).

7. In LSD therapy sessions, the therapist often lets the person's processes continue without heavy-handed intervention or interpretation. The most relevant unconscious elements and material usually emerge readily and spontaneously. "Because of this unusual property, LSD can be used as a kind of 'inner radar' that scans the unconscious, identifies the areas of high affective tension, and brings them to the open. . . . The phenomenology of LSD sessions thus reflects the key problems of the subject and exposes the roots and sources of his emotional difficulties on the psychodynamic, perinatal, and transpersonal levels" (Grof, 1975, p. 216).

8. When a young adult has a schizophrenic episode, the traditional model of treatment tries to control and abort the episode. John W. Perry, in contrast, established a center called Diabasis to provide a close trusting relationship so that the schizophrenic episode could continue and be supported. He views such episodes as an attempt at self-healing. The therapist allows the person's natural process to unfold, and does not try to take over control of that process. As one Diabasis staff member said, "What is called madness can best be understood as a journey of exploration and discovery, regulated by the psyche, in which the various elements of the personality can be reorganized in a more fruitful and self-fulfilling way" (B. Heller, quoted in Rogers, 1977, p. 25).

9. In some approaches to therapy or personal growth, the professional helper guides the process but not the content. In fact, the helper may not know what content the person is dealing with at the time, and even afterwards may not find out. In a journal workshop,

for instance, the participants may not be asked to share the content of their writing. In some psychosynthesis exercises the content is controlled by the person's subconscious or higher self, not by the therapist. A primal therapist once explained to me that he often has to sit patiently beside the client for an hour at a time without knowing the content of the client's highly emotional and dramatic process.

10. That same primal therapist tries to teach his clients how to deal with primal experiences so they can then do this on their own. In fact, one of the major outcomes of the widespread human growth movement may simply be that people develop a repertoire of techniques and exercises from which they can choose in future when faced with a problem. Whenever I discuss this notion with my graduate classes, I am impressed by the number of persons who use journal writing, informal cocounseling, dream work, topdog-underdog dialogues, self-guided fantasies, and cathartic emotional expression for dealing with various emotional crises and personal problems. No wonder the theme "Power to the Person" was chosen for one of the annual meetings of the Association for Humanistic Psychology!

11. Many self-help books, too, provide suggestions, exercises, and techniques for use when appropriate. Some self-help books try to overcontrol the person's process, but others offer a variety of suggestions from which the person can choose. *The Dream Game* by Faraday (1976), for instance, outlines three broad ways of working with dreams, rather than a single tightly controlled path.

12. In some approaches to human growth, the content itself emphasizes the power and adequate self-image of the person. I remember Virginia Satir at one workshop drawing three diagrams to illustrate interaction in which (1) I erase myself, (2) I erase the other person, (3) we are both okay. The TA phrase "I'm OK, you're OK" captures a similar stance. Assertiveness training, too, encourages us to stand up for our own rights and needs, but without putting down the other person. In couple communication, the most effective orientation is "I count and I count you—we both count" (Miller, Nunnally, and Wackman, 1975).

13. Peer self-help groups for those with addictions, mental health problems, and emotional crises are rapidly spreading. Groups exist for battered wives, addicted gamblers, alcoholics,

schizophrenics, overweight persons, drug addicts, parents of children with cancer, persons in debt, stutterers, divorced persons, families and individuals with emotional problems, people afraid of flying, former patients of mental institutions, people with high IQs, ex-offenders, parents of children who have died of Sudden Infant Death Syndrome, parents of autistic children, neurotics, parents of abused children, families of prisoners, people with phobias, facially disfigured persons, and widows (Gartner and Riessman, 1977, app. A). Professional helpers are involved at times with some of these groups, but are rarely permitted to overcontrol them. Professionals in several fields are struggling to work out appropriate forms of interaction with self-help groups.

14. The mental patients' liberation movement has documented the inappropriate uses of involuntary commitment, and the ways some mental patients are treated. "Occasional instances of kindness and compassion stand out in sharp contrast to overwhelming isolation and contempt imposed by most forms of 'treatment.' We came together to express our anger and despair at the way we were treated. Out of that process has grown the conviction that we *must* set up our own alternatives, because nothing that currently exists or is proposed fundamentally alters the unequal power relationships that are at the heart of the present mental health system. Power, not illness or treatment, is what the system is all about. It is a power that usually is not spoken about. (Patients who do are often labeled 'paranoid.')" (Chamberlin, 1978, p. xiii). Chamberlin's book also describes some of the genuine alternatives that have been developed for helping people experience great emotional pain and distress.

15. Some psychotherapists and mental hospitals are experimenting with written treatment contracts. During the negotiation process, the patient plays an active role in choosing the problems, treatment goals, and treatment methods. Responsibility is more shared than in traditional psychotherapy. "The participants perform roles that are more equal than is general in the early phase of the therapeutic encounter. Because they are engaged in a common task which demands responsibilities from each, the process conforms to many of the principles of consumerism. That is, the patient is encouraged to behave as someone who has rights, is seeking a service and has to make a series of choices and decisions about the treatment he is offered" (Rosen, 1978, p. 413).

## Social Work

Some social workers, instead of themselves being largely in charge of the client's changes, are now working with natural neighborhood helpers, natural support systems such as relatives and neighbors, and mutual help networks. Several of these exploratory ventures have been described by Collins and Pancoast (1974) and by Caplan and Killilea (1976). I was impressed by the size and enthusiasm of a 1980 conference on this theme at the University of Toronto (Shapiro, 1980).

Another important but much narrower approach is to work only with face-to-face groups that meet at scheduled times. These peer self-help or mutual aid groups have been thoroughly examined by Gartner and Riessman (1977) and by Lieberman and others (1979).

The dramatic effects of relating authentically to handicapped children at a summer camp, and encouraging them to break free from imposed activities, are movingly portrayed by Ron Jones (1977).

## Adult Learning

Certain shifts from professional overcontrol to shared responsibility are evident in continuing education, management development, professional and staff development, parent education, and other areas of adult education. The need for these shifts has been well documented during the past few years.

The process of self-planned learning has been recognized as widespread and successful in a recent research review (Tough, 1979, postscript). This review of more than 20 research studies pointed out that the learner makes the day-to-day decisions on what and how to learn in 73% of all adult learning efforts. An early study of such learning efforts found that the learner could recall actively performing a median of nine different teaching and planning tasks, such as setting the learning goals and planning the strategy, in each learning effort (Tough, 1967). About 7% of the adult's learning projects are planned by a friend, neighbor, or other nonprofessional. These figures mean that only about 20% of all intentional learning efforts by adults are planned and guided by professionals. About 10% rely on a professionally led group, 7% rely on individual instruction from a professional, and 3% rely largely on the guidance provided by a book or other nonhuman resource.

In a national survey of the United States, Penland (1977, p. 32) studied the reasons people have when they choose to learn on their own instead of taking a course. Here are the four reasons that were most often selected as particularly important from a list of ten:

1. desire to set my own learning pace
2. desire to use my own style of learning
3. I wanted to keep the learning style flexible and easy to change.
4. desire to put my own structure on the learning project

To me, it is highly significant that every one of these common reasons reflects the issue of control. In all four reasons the person wants to retain control and retain his or her own natural process, not have a professional instructor take over. The other six reasons in this study were selected less often, and do not particularly reflect the issue of control. Adult educators traditionally say people lack money and transportation for attending courses, but these two reasons ranked last.

In a report for the U.S. government, Ziegler concluded that "society, in all of its structures and institutions of human interaction, should remain sufficiently open, participatory and pluralistic to enable a robust, noncentralized, highly diversified system of adult learning to flourish. That conclusion suggests that public policy should *not* aim at supporting lifelong learning, for historically public policy support has led to *prescribing, limiting,* and *rendering compulsory* the human activities on which it focuses" (1977a, p. i). He urged that public dollars be allocated to organizations or programs according to how well they nurture adults' competencies in planning and evaluating their own learning, and promote their interest in further learning.

In an important synthesis called *The Missing Link,* Cross (1978) examined the question of what should be done to foster and facilitate adult learning even more than society does now. According to her, the fundamental issue in this debate is the question of who should have the primary responsibility for planning and directing the entire adult learning enterprise: (1) educators, planners, and organizations or (2) individual adult learners. "If one wished to find some middle ground on which to base agreement . . . most people could probably rally around the concept of self-planned learning for adults. Self-planned learning implies that the learner makes the decisions about learning goals, selecting from a wide variety of materials and resources those that best fit his or her goals" (pp. 3–4).

In 1976, the U.S. Congress passed a Lifelong Learning Act, and in 1978 the first annual report under that act was published (Lifelong Learning Project, 1978). After describing various concepts of lifelong learning, the report stated that "the problem with all these views of lifelong learning is that they focus on programs rather than on learning and learners. In this report, *lifelong learning* refers to the process by which individuals continue to develop their knowledge, skills, and attitudes over their lifetimes. . . . All deliberate learning activities are included, whether they occur in the workplace, the home, through formal or nonformal organizations, through traditional or nontraditional methods, or through the self-directed efforts of the individual himself or herself" (pp. 1–2). The report urges "greater emphasis on learners and their learning in government policies, programs, and research" (p. 5). Although the federal government is already heavily involved in adult learning, "the Lifelong Learning Act signals a promising shift in emphasis and perspective. Instead of stressing institutions, degrees, and programs labeled 'education,' it speaks of people, how they learn, what they learn, and where they learn. It considers the things people need to learn throughout their lives in order to survive, cope, be happy and productive, love, and grow old with dignity" (p. 18).

In 1979, Unesco convened a meeting of "European experts on the forms of autonomous learning" in Paris. At that meeting, I was impressed by the widespread interest and experimentation in shifting from classroom teacher control to individual learner participation in the responsibility for pace, methods, and content.

Let us move now to the more specific level: some examples of the shift from high professional control to shared responsibility.

1. Although only about 10% of adult learning efforts are guided by an instructor in a group, this is the stereotype of adult learning that first comes to mind. Also, it is this situation that many professional adult educators first think of changing when they want to shift toward greater sharing of responsibility. Several of their approaches are labeled "self-directed learning" although, in fact, they vary somewhat. Roger Harrison (1977) has successfully provided self-directed learning opportunities for groups of managers and administrators in large organizations. Each participant is encouraged to initiate (or withdraw from) any activity in order to meet his or her own needs. In addition, each person is free to manage his or her individual cycle of moving back and forth between risk/stress and reflection/integration. "We believe that the freedom self-directed

learning gives to follow this stress management cycle is a major reason why our programs can deal with highly charged and deeply personal material with a much lower level of stress than is true of more 'groupy' programs" (p. 87). An unpublished paper by Joffre Ducharme movingly described his success with a self-directed approach to learning in a one-week management workshop with first-line supervisors in Canada's taxation department. Early in the week each supervisor was encouraged to select specific change goals, and then he or she spent the rest of the week using various human and nonhuman resources to achieve these individual goals. In working with groups of illiterates, Paulo Freire (1970) did not arrive with a set of curriculum, but instead helped the people discover words with special meaning and power for them. Several other approaches to self-directed learning occur in university credit courses for adults, and will be described in the following section on higher education.

2. Any workshop or course, regardless of its format, can encourage the participants to continue their learning after the course is finished. In the United States, for instance, the Executive Development Department of Westinghouse Electric Corporation has developed a large form for participants in a three-week program for general managers. Called a continuing personal development plan, this worksheet has four columns. The instructions explain that "the *subject* column is for listing where you want to go—the area where you perceive a significant gap in your level of competence. The *sources/resources* column is to identify how you are going to get there. You might want to list books or articles you may know about, a seminar or course that might be valuable, people you may want to talk to. *Strategies and time frame* is where you spell out the what and when. The *evidence of attainment* column is where you may want to list indicators you will use to judge 'when you have arrived.' These indicators might take the form of operational results, personal evaluations, or evaluations by others." In Canada, at their three-day course in essentials of management, Commonwealth Holiday Inns of Canada provide each learner with a self-assessment instrument and a form for listing changes to be implemented after the course.

3. For evaluating proposed or actual programs in lifelong learning, Ziegler (1977b) has developed a fascinating 30-item instrument. The items rate the extent to which the program enhances or inhibits the following: the learner's responsibility for choosing his

or her learning goals and strategies, the learner's competence at planning and evaluating learning, and the learner's future enthusiasm and opportunities for learning.

4. Individual learning contracts are being used more and more for continuing professional development. A learning contract spells out the person's goals and strategies (and perhaps the methods for evaluating achievement) for one major learning project. A federally funded project in Kansas enabled mental health professionals to develop and carry through their own learning contracts. Details of this project have been reported in the various issues of *Self-Directed Professional Development Newsletter* and in Keeney (1980).

Individual learning contracts also make good sense as one option for professionals who must undertake continuing education in order to retain their professional license or certificate, or in order to maintain or improve their salary level. In some states and professions, recognition is given to individual self-directed learning as well as courses and workshops. Cooper and her committee (1978) have developed a useful document for use by state licensing and continuing education approval bodies. To alleviate the feeling of being locked in by an approved learning contract, their document states that "as the learner carries out the project, the proposed plan may be modified. Expected outcomes or objectives may change [as a result of] new developments or expanded knowledge. Learner's needs or interests may change. . . . Such changes (with rationale) should be incorporated into the final report, but they do not require renegotiation with the approval body" (p. 5).

Individual learning contracts are also used more and more within university credit programs, as we shall see in the section on higher education.

5. In Nancy, France, a person who wants to learn any aspect of English for any purpose is given an excellent range of options at the Centre de Recherches et d'Application Pédagogiques En Langues (Stanchina, 1976). The person chooses his or her own combination of helper, outside help, simulation, task matching, peer matching, personal reading materials, friends and neighbors who speak English, cassettes, written texts, and a sound library. Each helper in the center is skilled at diagnosing particular linguistic difficulties and at suggesting appropriate methods. At the 1979 Unesco meeting on autonomous learning, I did not hear of any other language center or system that gave learners as wide a choice of options. In my opin-

ion, this general approach could be very useful for helping people learn many other types of subject matter too.

6. Learning networks, such as The Learning Exchange serving Evanston and the greater Chicago area (Lewis and Kinishi, 1977), are very close to the learner-control end of the continuum. They do not try to control either the goals or the methods of learning. Instead, they simply provide the names and telephone numbers of persons who can serve as helpers with whatever sort of learning or change the caller wishes. Thousands of learners and helpers have been matched by the successful learning networks.

7. A few agencies are experimenting with group support and stimulation for self-planned projects. Ronald Gross is exploring the possibility of developing centers in major American cities for advanced scholars who are not working at a university or similar institution. In San Francisco, the Humanistic Psychology Institute has launched three mentor programs. According to their 1980 brochure, "the programs are patterned after the medieval mentor-student relationship. . . . The core of the Mentor Program is the working group, composed of the mentor and fellows. Fellows pursue creative individual projects of their choosing; the mentor serves to guide, support, and facilitate these projects. . . . The working group provides the fellows with the opportunity to meet others of like mind and commitment, thus giving valuable support and shared feedback for the mutual realization of their goals."

## Higher Education

We turn now to shifts in colleges and universities from high instructor control to shared responsibility. Before examining several recent examples, though, let us briefly note that other examples have a long history. Over the decades, some instructors have given their students a free choice of topic or focus for essays, projects, and other assignments. Many theses and dissertations have been examples of shared responsibility. On many campuses, students have had an option of taking one or two individual reading courses or independent study courses. Some academic advisors have helped students clarify their goals before choosing appropriate courses.

In recent years, some additional efforts to reduce instructor control have been implemented. Although somewhat diverse at first glance, these efforts have one thing in common: an attempt to shift from a high degree of control by the instructor, from an attitude of "the instructor knows best," to greater choice and control in the hands of the students. The responsibility for choosing what and how to learn is partially shifted away from the instructor. It may be shifted to a set of materials, to the individual learner, to small groups of learners, or to the whole class.

1. Sometimes the detailed control over what and how to learn resides in a set of tape recordings or programmed instruction materials, often called "individualized instruction." Most of these pre-programmed materials shift only two sorts of responsibility to the learner: when to learn and at what pace.

2. Competency-based degree programs have become common in recent years. The competencies required for the degree are spelled out, along with assessment procedures for judging when the student has gained each competency. "The competency-based program has as one of its features a separation of the learning processes from the assessment or certification process, a separation of teacher from assessor. . . . It gives responsibility to different persons for planning and monitoring the two phases" (Josephs, 1978, p. 13). In my opinion, basing credentials and hiring on demonstrated competencies (not on how the person gained the knowledge and skill) is a giant step toward freeing up higher education. The important question of who should decide the appropriate competencies was raised by Daloz (1978). He urged that students be encouraged to write their own competence statements, which may differ from those of other students. Adjusting to such diversity of learning may be painful for the college or university: "It must be willing to take the chance that its 'products' will differ widely from one another, recognizing that 'quality control' is not necessarily synonymous with 'content control' " (p. 26).

3. In a few colleges and universities, students are helped to learn how to set goals and plan their strategies, and generally "learn how to learn." Robert Smith has written a comprehensive paper (1976) on this topic and provides workshops for his students on learning how to learn. A project in England experimented extensively with a variety of approaches to increasing the capacity of students to organize their own learning. These approaches included conversations to help students develop and clarify their own natural language for talking about the purposes, strategies, outcomes, and evaluation of their learning efforts. The report on this project concluded that

"even a small shift in emphasis from teaching to systematically encouraging the development of learning skill would produce a massive educational pay off. . . . Learning-to-Learn should become a central theme. . . . Whether changes in the destiny of humans is brought about by Malthusian type checks or by wisdom or foresight, depends largely on the experience we now offer for learning-to-learn in the classrooms, lecture rooms, studies and laboratories of our educational institutions" (Thomas and Harri-Augstein, 1977, p. 211).

4. Ginny Griffin has developed a highly effective self-directed approach to teaching in her graduate courses. Early in the course she brings differences in learning style and philosophy to the surface through questionnaires and discussion. Throughout the course she increasingly leaves the responsibility for decision-making with the students. Because of her reputation as an excellent teacher, however, some students initially expect her to be strongly in control. As Griffin put it in a highly insightful review of self-directed learning (1978, 1979): "So people come, expecting me to 'do it to them,' to watch the master at work. After about nine hours together, they begin to realize that although I am going to be fully engaged, whatever good that's going to happen to them, they have to make happen themselves. That point of realization used to be called 'dump the professor' night. Now that I'm aware of the process, and try to prepare us all for it, it is more subtly known as the moment when 'the penny drops.' People have taken on responsibility for what happens to them" (1979, p. 13). The students' experiences with Griffin's approach have been described in detail by Bates (1979).

5. Malcolm Knowles (1975, pp. 44–58) has described his approach to a 15-session graduate course. Before and during the third session, each student develops a learning contract, which can subsequently be revised or renegotiated as the student's interests change or become clearer. Certain knowledge and skill that most students have included in their contracts is handled by small groups ("inquiry teams"), who make class presentations during the eighth meeting through the thirteenth meeting. At the end of the course, each student is allotted up to 45 minutes to present evidence, to two peers, of having accomplished his or her objectives.

6. Originally trained as a school teacher, I believed the instructor should control almost all decisions about what and how stu-

dents learn. Later, though, as I listened to more and more interviewees tell me about their highly successful and enthusiastic learning outside of educational institutions, I began to question my own teaching approach in my graduate courses. Perhaps the students would learn more relevant knowledge and skill, and learn it more effectively, if I allowed their course learning to resemble their real-life learning (Tough, 1979, chaps. 10 and 14). As I have let this occur over the years, my teaching has evolved into a rather unusual approach, but it works well for me and for the particular students in the particular graduate courses I teach.

I definitely retain *some control* over what and how students learn. I continue to have some definite structure, requirements, and boundaries even though I keep these to a minimum. I stay within the range of instructor control that is most effective for student learning, but I try to keep near the lower end of that range. I largely control the overall sequence of topics and activities for class sessions and provide brief lectures and other input. Although I facilitate the discussion and group process, I do so with a light hand and without trying to control the detailed content. In order to pass the course, students are required to spend at least 120 hours (more for higher grades) at highly deliberate learning efforts that are clearly within the subject matter boundaries of the course. They also must read 15 books (more for higher grades) from my 60-item course bibliography: they then rate these books, and when I revise the bibliography I am guided largely by their votes. These requirements are negotiable by individual students after they have spent two weeks trying to operate within them.

Within the structure just described, each student has complete *freedom of what and how to learn.* In the 90 hours of learning outside the classroom, each student is largely free to plan and modify an individual learning path. In a sense there are 18 different individual courses within the one graduate course if there are 18 students in the class. I urge the students not to plan too far ahead: their interests, questions, and activities are bound to change as they gain new ideas and experiences early in the course. Class sessions serve largely to open up topics for the students, to provide support and enthusiasm for their individual learning paths, and to provide a safe haven where their difficulties and adventures and new thoughts can be heard sympathetically. I have virtually no power to control the student's grade, and am therefore perceived primarily as a helper or a facilitator of learning with whom the student can be completely honest, open, and vulnerable without fear of receiving a lower grade as a result.

In my experience, it is not enough for an instructor to set a minimum amount of structure and then to give students plenty of freedom with what and how to learn. In addition, students need *access to plenty of help and resources.* This help is not compulsory and has no strings attached. I became aware of the enormous amount of help that people receive during real-life self-planned learning in my first research study (Tough, 1967), in which I found that the adult receives help from an average of 10.6 individuals during a single learning project. Class sessions provide support and energy, and also help students choose their individual directions. I encourage students to discuss their particular interests with other students in the class who have similar interests, and even to find a learning partner for the entire course from within the class or elsewhere. Exercises, a list of individual interests, coffee breaks, and class discussion all help students discover appropriate resources among the class members. The amount of human interaction is much higher with this teaching approach than in a traditional course. To help students choose and gain access to relevant books, I provide an annotated bibliography and lend my own books to students.

This approach unleashes a surprising amount of energy, enthusiasm, creativity, and diversity. The majority of students report that they read and learn more than in traditional courses. In Toronto, Vancouver, and North Carolina, students in my courses have used an amazing variety of methods and activities (far more than I could have ever suggested to them) to learn a wide variety of knowledge and skill. I treasure the diversity that is evident in their progress reports (they bring copies for everyone in the class) and in their final report to me (they describe the highlights of what and how they have learned).

My approach fails with a few students, however. They may expect and want a different approach, a different climate in the total group, or more time in smaller groups. They may be uncomfortable with the diversity of paths, and want the total group to reach agreement on goals and norms. They may like to engage in power struggles with their instructors, but cannot find a target against which to struggle within this approach.

7. Scott Armstrong has experimented with time contracts in five marketing courses at the Wharton School of the University of Pennsylvania. The students who selected this option kept a daily

diary on course activities, time spent, and knowledge and skill learned. Students who satisfied the instructor that they had spent between 100 and 124 hours at the course received a pass, those with 125–140 hours were graded as "high pass," and those over 140 hours were "distinguished." This approach encourages students to take responsibility for their own learning. "In addition, because the time contract eliminates the need to grade the student's output, it provides a better environment for learning" (J.S. Armstrong, 1980). Armstrong's data indicate that students using time contracts spent more time at learning, felt more responsible for their learning, and were more successful at changing attitudes and behavior, compared to their experiences under traditional teaching approaches.

8. Allender and Silberman (1979) experimented with three variations of student-directed learning. In one version the teacher structured various inquiry activities. A second variation emphasized learning in groups of peers. The third version was an individual mode, in which the student's learning was initiated by his or her own questions, and was organized by the student's own personal timetable. The individual mode was superior on some measures.

9. Most of the changes described so far involve a change within a course in which a group of students begin on a certain date to learn within one subject-matter area. In some colleges, however, students take few or no courses of this type. Instead, each student (in consultation with a faculty advisor or mentor) develops individual objectives and learning activities for each course. If groups of students meet at all, they do so to help and encourage and sometimes evaluate one another, not to learn or discuss content. Many colleges have permitted students to take one or two reading courses, individual study courses, independent study courses, or whatever that college calls an individually developed course. Only recently, though, have some colleges and universities expanded this approach to the student's entire program.

The McMaster University program (in Hamilton, Ontario) that produces medical doctors and other health professionals is one of the best and most widely known programs of individual learning. Much of the student's learning time is spent at individual needs and interests, both academic and practical. One medical student whom I interviewed, for instance, was the only person in her support group who needed to learn biochemistry. She was doing this on her own, with help when needed from one faculty member. The medical doctors produced by this program spend the last two months studying for nationwide examinations and achieve at least as well on the average as doctors trained in more traditional programs. This certainly points up the absurdity of a comment that I have heard several times after telling audiences about individual learning: "I certainly wouldn't want to use doctors or plumbers or car mechanics who taught themselves!"

Several colleges use individual learning contracts as their basic approach. By having program advisors in most major cities, Campus-Free College (now called Beacon College) has demonstrated the possibility of providing individual programs of study throughout the United States and Canada. Mark Cheren, one of the early leaders in Campus-Free College, produced a manual for the program advisors (1978b) and also studied the transition that students had to make from external direction in learning to greater self-direction in learning at Campus-Free College (1978a).

The section describing learning contracts in MacKenzie, Postgate, and Scupham (1975) described the three "systems of personalized study" at Empire State College, Minnesota Metropolitan State College, and the Community College of Vermont. The first of these has produced an interesting study of the role of the mentor in developing the individual learning projects (Bradley, 1975). Berte (1975), too, has provided useful insight into contract learning.

My only concern with learning contracts is the possibility that they sometimes produce a feeling of being locked in. Even when the student is told that the contract can be renegotiated anytime, I worry that having the objectives and learning activities spelled out on paper will produce a reluctance to reconsider and modify them. The need for flexibility throughout the learning was demonstrated when I asked David Yule to draw a diagram of his learning paths for one individual learning course he did with me. The diagram (reproduced in Keeney, 1980, p. 61) was intricate and complex. There is no way Yule could have sat down at the beginning and developed such a complex diagram. Even more important, his interests and questions and directions kept changing as he went along, because his knowledge and perspective and inquiry kept changing. After all, that is what inquiry and learning are all about!

Holland College in Prince Edward Island provides partially individual personalized programs for its students. One feature is the highly specific analysis of possible learning objectives for each career field that the college provides. This detailed chart of possible objectives helps students choose their optional objectives and learning activities, and also serves as a basis for evaluation and as a record of achievement. In fact, this chart serves as the student's "diploma," and can show potential employers exactly what knowledge and skills the student has learned.

Such a chart might be useful during job-hunting for the person who has deliberately learned for two or three years without attending college at all. Coyne and Hebert (1972, p. 127) suggested that such persons develop a bound portfolio that includes descriptions or papers they have written.

10. Giving academic credit for learning that occurs at work, as a homemaker, or in other real-life situations is another movement that reduces professional control. Houle (1973) has documented this "third generation" of degree programs for adults. The publications of the Council for the Advancement of Experiential Learning have described various approaches in detail.

## Elementary and Secondary Education

Although this book focuses largely on adults, some of the findings and implications probably apply to adolescents and perhaps even to younger children. Briefly, then, let us examine secondary and elementary education.

For at least 40 years, some schools and teachers have experimented with a shift from high teacher control to shared responsibility. Many teachers encourage students to choose a topic or project of interest for an assignment or essay within one course. Some teachers set the learning objectives, but leave students free to choose their own methods and resources. In some schools, students may choose individual or independent study for an entire course.

The Association for Supervision and Curriculum Development established a Project on Self-Directed Learning in 1977 and published a book focusing specifically on that approach in 1979. The book opens with the following declaration: "In a democratic society, students need to have opportunities to learn how to choose *what* is to be learned, *how* it is to be learned, *when* it is to be learned, and *how to evaluate* their own progress" (Della-Dora and Blanchard, 1979, p. 1). The opening chapter describes what one finds (1) toward the school-directed end of the continuum, (2) at the shared responsibility ("self-directed") position on the continuum, and (3) at a point midway between these two positions in each of the following areas: deciding what is to be learned, selecting methods and materials for learning, communicating with others about what is being learned, and evaluating achievement of goals.

Gibbons and Phillips (1978) described the crises and difficulties for both teachers and students when making a transition from teacher-directed to self-directed learning. After describing several phases characteristic of students who are making this transition, the authors suggest specific strategies for each phase. "Whatever the difficulties involved, it is important that students learn to direct their own education before they leave school. . . . We believe that no educational institution—whether kindergarten or graduate school—has completed its task until its students have demonstrated their ability to plan and implement their own learning programs" (p. 300).

There is a small but growing trend among parents to educate their children at home, at least in the United States. For these children, this is a major step away from high control by the professional educational establishment, although it is also possible for parents to overcontrol. According to Harris (1979), more than 700 parents subscribe to John Holt's *Growing Without Schools* newsletter, and the Council for Educational Freedom in America has launched a campaign to halt state-ordered schooling. Although 32 states have some statutory provision for alternatives to attending school, court battles sometimes occur regarding the quality or standards of the home education.

## Library Practice

In recent years, some librarians have been giving particular attention to their clients' natural process of changing, learning, or seeking information, and have been trying to fit into that process more effectively. Some librarians are increasingly seeing themselves as a learning consultant, a helper, a counselor, or a highly flexible link between the client and various information systems and sources.

An intensive study by Carr (1979) of the interaction between librarians and their clients underlines the importance of this shift. His study concluded that the following librarian characteristics, along with several others, were especially important in distinguishing helpful episodes from unhelpful episodes: (a) ability to attend to and know the learner as an individual with an inquiry unlike any other, (b) willingness to explore all potential courses of inquiry, guided by a standard of optimal fit, and (c) sensitivity to the learner's need for self-esteem, autonomy, reassurance, and competence (p. 221).

## Religion

For some people, the largest intentional change during their adult years is their spiritual growth. For example, they become closer to God, they seek mystical experiences, they are baptized in the Holy Spirit, or they develop insights into the ultimate meaning of life and the universe. Although a remarkably large number of people are turning to the established religions these days, many other people are following their own paths. On their own or with friends, without help from a religious professional, they meditate, pray, seek God in wilderness solitude or by the ocean, experience cosmic union through psychedelic drugs, create their own religious rituals, seek ultimate meaning through myths or dreams or reading, or pursue mystical experiences through such means as music, chanting, or sex. Wickett's (1977) conception of spiritual growth became wider and wider as his interviewees told him about a surprising variety of personal paths for religious and spiritual change.

Another significant intentional change for many of us is entering into marriage. It is fascinating that to be married we typically turn to a religious professional (priest, minister, rabbi, etc.). Some persons, however, are now planning or writing part of their own marriage ceremony. A small but growing number are choosing to live together without going through a legal or religious service. A few of these hold an unofficial ceremony or celebration with friends and relatives.

## Families

I regard parents as quasi-professional helpers with their child's intentional changes. They are designated by social custom, even by law, as the persons responsible for helping their children to change and develop in certain ways. In fact, too, most parents play significant roles in many of their child's changes.

Many parents overcontrol their children. In stores, parks, and streets, I am amazed at the number of commands and criticisms parents direct at their children.

Other parents provide a definite contrast, fortunately. They love their children as they are, and help them choose and achieve the goals and changes that the children want. They fit into each child's particular process of change, growth, unfolding, goal-setting, play, and learning. They provide a good balance of freedom and control, with plenty of help and resources available for the child's use. If these parents make a decision that affects the child, they will usually give the child plenty of information about the decision and the reasons for it.

Around the middle of this century, according to DeMause (1974), a new mode of parent-child relationships became evident in some families. DeMause called this the helping mode, and he compared it to the socialization mode of the preceding century and a half and the intrusive mode of the eighteenth century. "The helping mode involves the proposition that the child knows better than the parent what it needs at each stage of its life, and fully involves both parents in the child's life as they work to empathize with and fulfill its expanding and particular needs. There is no attempt at all to discipline or form 'habits.' Children are neither struck nor scolded, and are apologized to if yelled at under stress" (p. 52). DeMause has suggested that this sort of parent-child relationship "results in a child who is gentle, sincere, never depressed, never imitative or group-oriented, strong-willed, and unintimidated by authority" (p. 54).

A widely learned approach to child-raising in recent years has been Thomas Gordon's "Parent Effectiveness Training." Gordon (1970) has clearly confronted the issue of power and control. He has spelled out a method of conflict resolution in which child and parent cooperate as partners in a joint search for a solution acceptable to both of them. Gordon called this "a no-power method—or more accurately a 'no-lose' method: conflicts are resolved with no one winning and no one losing. Both win because *the solution must be acceptable to both*" (p. 196). The results are in marked contrast to the battles that occur in the many households in which one or both parents exert power over the child (or in the smaller number of families in which the children are allowed all the power and the parents usually give in).

Gordon has also discussed another type of situation, in which the child's behavior or beliefs do not interfere with the parent's rights or goals in any concrete tangible way. For example, the child or adolescent may believe strongly in the right to choose his or her own friends, values, clothing style, and hair length. Parents sometimes have difficulty at first in accepting Gordon's "principle of allowing the child freedom to become what he wants to become, provided his behavior does not tangibly and concretely interfere with the parent becoming what he wants to become" (p. 273). The P.E.T. approach helps parents handle this situation by modeling their own values, and by offering themselves as a consultant to the child or teenager. As with consultants in the business world, however, the successful parent-consultant is first clearly "hired" by the child, "*shares* rather than preaches, *offers* rather than imposes, *suggests* rather than demands. Even more critical, the successful consultant shares, offers, and suggests usually no more than *once*. . . . The successful consultant offers his ideas, then *leaves responsibility with his client* for *buying* or *rejecting them*" (pp. 275–276). What a contrast to the hard-sell approach and constant hassling used by most parents to try to change their child's values, clothes, hair length, or lifestyle!

Richard Farson is interested in reducing not only parental overcontrol but also parental guilt at not successfully changing their children into the exact ideal person of the parent's dreams. In *Birthrights* (1974, p. 15), Farson has said that "parents need to be freed from the burden of guilt that comes from believing that they are solely responsible for what their children become." He has also claimed that the hundreds of books giving advice on how to raise children have one overwhelming problem: "They convey the erroneous idea that it is indeed possible to raise children; that there is a way to do it; that one can successfully manage, control, stimulate, and motivate them; that one can make them creative, well-mannered, healthy, adjusted, informed, and aspiring; and that one can discharge these responsibilities with judgment, taste, style, contentment, intelligence, and a minimum of frustration and doubt. What the books don't tell is that being a good parent isn't just difficult, it's impossible. There is simply no way to be a good parent in a society organized against children" (p. 13).

In 1975, Howell pointed out the advantages of each family's relying on itself and on networks instead of relying unduly on institutional and professional help. Here is her position: "I believe that our families could thrive by: (1) working to develop trusting relationships with a wide human network of kin, friends, neighbors, and others with whom we feel a sense of community; (2) insisting that 'experts' share with us the knowledge and skills that we need to conduct our own affairs; (3) utilizing the paid services of professionals at our own convenience—that is, only when *we* wish to do so, and on *our* terms" (p. xiii).

## Personal Liberation Movements

In personal liberation movements that have flourished since 1960, many people have developed their feelings of self-esteem, competence, power, and success. Some of the movements also preach that their members do not have to be "dependent upon systems purporting to meet their 'needs' through individualized professional help" (McKnight, 1977, p. 80). In fact, some movements explicitly reject the views of professionals as erroneous and damaging.

The women's liberation movement helps women sense and treasure their power, competence, success, self-worth, importance, skills, talents, strengths, and contributions. It helps each woman take control of her life, discover and choose the paths that suit her, and become more assertive in gaining her own rights and goals. She is encouraged to stand up for herself as a full-fledged person when dealing with professionals such as lawyers, therapists, loan officers, and medical doctors. It is significant that the women's liberation movement, which I see as the most successful adult change enterprise of the past 20 years, relies largely on peers and volunteers rather than professionals. Some researchers, such as Posluns (1981), are using intensive interviews with women to study the natural change process of becoming free of sex-role stereotyping in attitudes and behavior.

Children, probably more than any other groups, are dramatically overcontrolled. Children suffer from "the root pathology of human relationship in all but the simplest, most egalitarian human societies: the drive to dominate, to mold the other. . . . Most western adults would not dare talk to their peers the way they talk to children or to their elderly parents. Nor would they themselves accept the interruptions, corrections, demands for attentiveness and instant displays of affection that children accept as a matter of course" (Boulding, 1979a, p. 6). In his book on birthrights (1974, p. 27), Farson stated that "children, like adults, should have the right to decide the matters which affect them most directly. The issue of self-determination is at the heart of children's liberation. It is, in fact, the only issue, a definition of the entire concept. . . . Children would, for example, have the right to exercise self-determination in decisions about eating, sleeping, playing, listening, reading, washing, and dressing. They would have the right to choose their associates, the opportunity to decide what life goals they wish to pursue, and the freedom to engage in whatever activities are permissible for adults." Boulding presented a similar theme: "The theme of all human rights covenants, and the motif of all liberation movements, is participation in the shaping of one's own life and that of the society around one, and reasonable access to resources that will make that participation possible" (1979a, p. 7).

Several of the personal liberation movements are refusing to let psychiatrists, psychotherapists, clergy, or other professional helpers define them as deficient, abnormal, or mentally ill. Some former mental patients are organizing against oppression and negative definitions. Gay persons, though no longer officially classified by psychiatrists as mentally ill, must still struggle against being perceived and treated this way by some professional helpers. Some professionals even deny the existence of certain types of people that do, in fact, exist, such as those with bisexual preferences or with psychic sensitivity. Klein's book (1978) has contributed to the recognition and liberation of bisexual persons, and "psychic lib" groups in California are helping psychically sensitive people to accept and treasure their special abilities.

## Governments and Society

Until now, this chapter has dealt largely with the interaction between a helping professional (or paraprofessional or parent) and the changing person. Some helpers are shifting from high control to shared responsibility. Some parallel shifts are occurring in the broader spheres of government and politics, economics, and society in general. In this final section, let us examine this broader context.

Two powerful but conflicting movements are gaining momentum in several countries today. On the one hand is the vigorous effort by various levels of government and by credentialed helpers to gain greater influence, information, diagnostic and decision-making power, and responsibility. Government programs, child abuse agencies, mental health professionals, departments of defense and war, and the medical establishment are all expanding their sphere of influence, or at least fighting strongly to do so. On the other hand is an equally vigorous effort by various groups fostering the awareness, competence, liberty, power, and responsibility of the individual person. They believe in tolerating or even encouraging the diversity of goals, lifestyles, religions, and personal mistakes that occur when people can choose freely from a range of opportunities and resources.

I am deeply impressed by the power of each of these opposing movements. Each is energetic, widely supported, and gaining some new ground. I see the clash between them as a major theme in many countries during the next 15 years. At the First Global Conference on the Future in July 1980, I presented a paper on this topic and found that a high proportion of the audience agreed strongly with the topic's significance.

In this chapter, we have already seen several examples of both movements. Let us end this survey with some examples, at the broad societal and governmental level, of the shift from high control to greater individual responsibility. A few of these examples are too extreme to win my wholehearted approval, but I believe it is important to note them as part of the broader context within which to consider the earlier parts of this chapter. Each example is a reflection of our central theme.

1. In the United States, the United Kingdom, and Canada, some efforts have already succeeded in limiting government spending or taxation, the size of government bureaucracy, and (through sunset laws) the duration of legislation and government programs without renewal. Additional efforts are in progress. For instance, the National Taxpayers Union has sparked a drive to get state legislatures to mandate the U.S. Congress to call a national convention to propose a constitutional amendment requiring a balanced federal budget. Further, the National Tax Limitation Committee has sponsored a draft amendment to limit spending at the federal level (Friedman and Friedman, 1980, p. 302).

2. The Libertarian party has become the third major political party in the United States, although it began only in 1971. Libertarian presidential candidate Ed Clark received about 920,000 votes in the 1980 election. In Canada, too, this party has been rapidly gaining ground. Although Libertarian candidates sometimes take extreme views on individual liberty, their positions do stimulate some people to think through their own position. The Libertarian platform opposes the various ways in which governments have allegedly interfered with the rights of people to manage their own lives and property. The major theoretical spokesperson for libertarianism has made the following claim: "While opposing any and all private or even group aggression against the rights of person and property, the libertarian sees that throughout history and into the present day, there has been one central, dominant, and overriding aggressor: the State. . . . The libertarian refuses to give the State the moral sanction to commit actions that almost everyone agrees would be immoral, illegal, and criminal if committed by any person or group in society" (Rothbard, 1978, p. 24).

3. Some parallel principles have been recommended by a psychologist, Will Schutz. Emphasizing individual awareness, self-determination, and self-responsibility throughout a recent book, Schutz developed the following principles for action (1979, pp. 144–146): The aim of any social institution should be the creation of social conditions within which individuals choose to find it easiest to determine their own lives. Permit any action done by an individual, with awareness, that does not impinge on another individual. Provide profoundly simple solutions to problems that individuals choose to have dealt with by institutions. Create conditions within which individuals are unlikely to block themselves from self-determination. Reward self-responsibility and awareness: do not accept obedience or lack of awareness as excuses.

4. Through a series of ten one-hour television programs called "Free to Choose" and a parallel book, Milton and Rose Friedman have aroused a great deal of interest in issues of individual liberty. The Friedmans applauded the principle of equality of opportunity and the liberty to shape one's own life. They suggested that personal liberty is bound to suffer when any government tries to achieve equality of *outcome*. Equality of outcome means that "everyone should have the same level of living or of income, should finish the race at the same time" or should at least receive "fair shares" (Friedman and Friedman, 1980, pp. 128, 135). "A society that puts equality—in the sense of equality of outcome—ahead of freedom will end up with neither equality nor freedom. The use of force to achieve equality will destroy freedom, and the force introduced for good purposes will end up in the hands of people who will use it to promote their own interests. On the other hand, a society that puts freedom first will, as a happy by-product, end up with both greater freedom and greater equality" (p. 148). During one of his television programs (April 9, 1980), Milton Friedman stated an idea that particularly impressed me: freedom is not the natural state of humankind, but is a rare and precious thing; it will take great courage and effort to stop being overgoverned.

5. In a highly influential book, Toffler foresees a rapid transition to "the third wave" characterized by a far more decentralized and diverse and participatory society, a de-massified society and the collapse of consensus, "a far more varied, colorful, open, and diverse society than any we have ever known," a democracy of shared minority power and "a fundamental devolution of power"

(1980, pp. 420, 424, 437, 454). Toffler urges us to support "thousands of conscious, decentralized experiments that permit us to test new models of political decision-making at the local and regional levels in advance of their application to the national and transnational levels" (p. 458).

6. Personal or psychological liberation is a major political issue, according to John Vasconcellos, successfully re-elected several times to the California Assembly. In an interview with Ken Dychtwald, Vasconcellos (1978, pp. 36–37) described a recent revolution in American politics: "Today the political issue that is emerging is for liberation at a psychological level: owning one's own body, mind, and feelings, and being one's self. This includes not passively surrendering ourselves and our power to some authority figure or institution who thinks they know better than we do who we ought to be." Vasconcellos distinguished five major steps in the revolutionary political developments of the last two decades (pp. 37–38): (1) a demystification of authority, moving away from the model in which someone other than us has all the power and authority; (2) breaking out of vertical authority models and shifting toward horizontal models in sharing of power, influence, and responsibility; (3) a movement toward individualization ("we're trying to change from a situation where we fix individuals to fit institutions, to organizing institutions whose function is to fit individuals"); (4) focusing attention and energy on the whole person in public and political policy-making; (5) "a movement toward empowerment—a real effort to evoke, encourage, and support in order to empower individual human beings to be healthy, whole, self-aware persons who are able to live horizontally without mystification and fear."

In much of his writing and speaking, Vasconcellos has underlined the significance of society's view of human nature. If we view people as untrustworthy and irresponsible, unable to make appropriate decisions about their own needs and lives, we will design political institutions and programs to shape, control, and repress. If we have greater faith in the person's capacity for self-direction, personal responsibility, and successful choice, our designs will be quite different. Based on this second set of beliefs, a new humanistic politics is beginning to emerge (Vasconcellos, 1979). Such a movement seems natural in nations based on a democratic form of government, which is built on a belief in the competence, power, and freedom of choice of the individual voter.

7. The New World Alliance has been quite important since it was founded in 1979 in the United States. This political organization (not a party) promotes self-reliance, human growth, a respect for diversity, personal responsibility for one's own behavior, convivial association and participation in decision-making processes, and voluntary certification to replace mandatory licensing (Governing Council of the New World Alliance, 1981).

8. In its approach to rural development, the Unesco plan for 1977–1982 has recognized the power and importance of the rural person's intentional change process. "Experience has shown that rural populations can mobilize their latent productivity for the sake of their own development, especially when they see some advantage to themselves in so doing. The men and women who are the goal of development must also be its agents. In view of this, it seems more and more obvious that rural community leaders and representatives must play a principal role in rural development" (Unesco, 1977, p. 248).

Turning specifically to rural education (adult and out-of-school education as well as schooling), the Unesco report again emphasized individual empowerment. "Education stands out as an essential component in any development program. It must first of all provide rural populations with the instruction that will enable them to make their voice heard and participate fully in the political, economic and social life of the nation" (p. 249).

9. *New Age* editor Peggy Taylor (1978, p. 4) has urged her readers to move from the level of personal individual empowerment to the world stage.

> The feelings of hopelessness and powerlessness that once enshrouded us in our personal lives have begun to fade in light of the increasing evidence to support the power of creative, positive attitudes in healing our bodies and our relationships. . . .
> We need to dare extend the metaphor of self-healing to a global dimension and to change some of our self-limiting assumptions about the world, taking inspiration from the small successes we have experienced in our personal lives. This means . . . daring to trust ourselves enough to express our heartfelt humanness in ever larger realms of society, not just in the safety of a circle of supportive friends. It means daring to expose

ourselves to people we may have thus far considered part of the problem. It means consciously testing out our own ability to make a difference, and knocking on some of the imaginary doors that we thought were shut against us.

There is no issue more important for us today than to cultivate a sense of personal responsibility toward the planet, and to learn to develop and trust in our personal power to create the kind of world we can gladly pass on to our children.

# Chapter 7

# Significant Directions for Research

In the two previous chapters we looked at some implications for improving practice that arise from the data of the first four chapters. I spelled out seven major directions for potential action over the next few years in hopes that these will stimulate readers to think of additional possibilities for their own situations.

Certain research directions, too, could contribute a great deal. As our knowledge and understanding of intentional changes increase, our policies and practices may become even more beneficial in fostering successful changes.

After careful thought, I have chosen the four directions for research that I believe will be most useful during the next few years. Each of these significant directions is outlined in one section.

## The Place of Intentional Changes Within All Changes

It would be useful and fascinating to study the place and relative importance of intentional changes within the person's total change over the years.

Let me use myself as an example for a moment. My total range of changes includes changes I have chosen and achieved intentionally, changes that other people managed intentionally to produce in me through their efforts and expectations, random chance external events over which I had little or no influence, unintended changes in my body, psychological development and maturation at various ages and stages, and changes in my ongoing stream of subconscious events (including dreams, fantasies, and symbols). How much has each type of change contributed to the differences between the person who is writing this and the Allen Tough of 10 or 20 years ago? How do the various types of changes interact and intermingle?

This could be a highly beneficial direction for research over the next decade. Our interview question (#10) and the discussion in chapters 1 and 3 barely scratch the surface of this whole area. In *Psychological Abstracts* and ERIC, however, I have not managed to find any other comprehensive research in this area.

Instead of studying the question at the most comprehensive level, researchers could begin with one or more particular areas. For example, what proportion of the person's changes over the years is intentional in each of the following areas: self-insight, effective satisfying human relationships, knowledge and understanding of the world, mental and physical health, job, child-raising approach, understanding of civic and political issues, recreational activities, altruistic efforts to contribute to others, major goals in life?

It would also be interesting to study the extent to which people vary. Are there two distinct types of people—reactors and searchers—as McGinnis (1975) suggested? Alternatively, are people arranged along a continuum from "most of my changes are intentional" to "most are unintentional"? How much do people vary from one year or decade of their life to another?

What sorts of people are generally at the two ends of the continuum? In chapter 3, when we looked at people with no intentional changes at all, we saw that they were often middle class and at a reasonably high educational level, not poor or deprived. Is this true of the population as a whole in each country, or was our sample highly unusual?

An interview schedule for comparing intentional and unintentional changes has recently been developed by Joan Neehall (1981). The interviewee is given handout sheets that provide detailed descriptions of eight areas of change. For each area in turn, the interviewee uses a four-point scale to rate the total size and importance of all changes within that area over the past four years. The person also selects the three most important areas of change. After receiving a careful explanation of intentional and unintentional, the interviewee reports the intentional percentage of the total change within each area in turn, and rates the benefit (to self and then to others) of the intentional and unintentional portions of each change area. The person is also asked to describe the content and process of the unintentional portion of each area. The interviewer then collects data on a wide range of personal variables in order to find out which ones vary between high changers and low changers, and between persons whose changes are largely unintentional and those who are largely intentional.

## Basic Surveys of Intentional Changes

The interviews conducted for this book have taken us a long way toward an accurate and comprehensive picture of intentional changes. There is also a clear need, however, for additional surveys and larger samples over the next few years. These could confirm or modify the figures presented in this book. In addition, various nations, subcultures, regions, ages, and occupational groups could be compared more thoroughly.

The basic data from each person will be the area of change, the percentage that was achieved, the size and importance of the change, and who performed the three major tasks. For these large-scale surveys, the supplementary questions at the end of the Appendix will probably be omitted and additional questions concerning personal and demographic variables will be added. A single-paragraph description of each of the nine areas of change could be useful as a probe for aiding recall, and could also be used by the interviewee to categorize his or her particular change. Questions 4 and 6 should be clarified to elicit either gross benefits or (my preference) net benefits. Also, question 11 could be improved by adding a four-point scale for the interviewee to rate the size of the additional change and how strongly it was wanted.

In order to obtain accurate data and a deep understanding of intentional changes, it is essential to use intensive, probing, medium-paced (almost leisurely at times), in-depth interviews. A quick interview in which the interviewer's main preoccupation is to jot down some data and then move on to another interview will simply not provide an accurate picture of an elusive complex phenomenon.

Doctoral students and other researchers interested in one particular area might want to study intentional changes in that particular area. For example, they could adapt the basic survey questions in the Appendix to cover intentional changes in any one of the following areas:

1. self-insight, emotions, and relationships,
2. job and career,
3. religion and spiritual growth,
4. philosophy of life, broad perspective on the meaning and purpose of life, and clarifying basic goals in life,
5. personality and behavior changes similar to those sought by therapists,
6. child-raising, marriage enrichment, and relating to members of one's household,
7. freedom from stereotyping in attitudes and behavior concerning sex roles or age roles,
8. ESP, astral travel, healing powers,
9. physical health and fitness,
10. giving up alcohol, gambling, crime, or child abuse,
11. managing one's time and life,
12. the researcher's process,
13. efforts to help others and contribute to the world.

Whether studying the total range of intentional changes or just the changes in one area of life, some researchers may want to try various definitions of the phenomenon. The changes that are recorded, and some of the other data, may vary according to the focus selected. For instance, one could focus on any one of the following:

1. the person's largest, most significant intentional change during the past two years (the focus of this book),
2. the largest intentional change during the past one, three, five, ten, or twenty years,
3. the two or three largest intentional changes during the given period,
4. all major intentional changes over the past two to ten years, or over several decades of the person's life, or over the entire lifetime,
5. the current change efforts that the person considers most important or to which the person is devoting the most effort or time.

## The Causes of Overcontrol

Another highly significant direction for further research is the causes of overcontrol in some helping relationships. During face-to-face interaction between a helper and another person, what factors and forces (both inner and outer) sometimes contribute to helper overcontrol and to the person's passive submission?

One section of the previous chapter was devoted to this question. It was highly speculative, however, rather than based on careful research. If research over the next few years illuminates this question, we may then develop even better strategies for encouraging both helper and client to operate more effectively.

## The Needs for Additional Help

From what additional help would people especially benefit? Research that successfully and precisely answered this question would be highly useful. Only by grasping the greatest unmet needs can helpers and institutions dramatically increase their effectiveness in fostering intentional changes. Insightful research along this line could lead to the provision of much better information, advice, services, materials, and helpers for intentional change. Only by discovering the gaps and unfilled needs can one be effective at filling them.

One key part of this research thrust will be to ask people directly about the additional help and resources and competence that would have been highly beneficial to them (questions 9D, 9E, and 9F in the Appendix). More precise answers to these questions are obtained if they are asked after the person has discussed a particular intentional change in some detail, rather than early in the interview.

It is also useful to ask about difficulties (question 6A) and about the major tasks performed by the person (questions 9A, 9B, and 9C). It is important to understand the person's entire natural process of intentional change, especially the tasks and help that already occur, and what goes wrong in that process. What forces repress change and limit the person's horizons? What are the greatest obstacles and barriers in the external world? What are the inner forces that produce self-deprecation, low awareness of thoughtfulness and success at previous changes, and willingness to submit readily to external authority? What goes wrong during the help-seeking process (see framework in Tough, 1979, chap. 10)? Where does the person stumble or almost quit? What mistakes does the person make? All of this information will provide an excellent foundation for thinking about what additional help, services, and resources to provide.

Some researchers may choose the concept of phases as their way of understanding and describing the process of intentional change. For example, Adams, Hayes, and Hopson (1976, chaps. 1 and 14) discuss phases as "a general model of transitions" (p. 8) and as "a *cycle* of reaction and feelings that is predictable" (p. 9). Research on phases may turn out to be fruitful, but my own preference is to use the three major tasks (choosing , planning, and implementing) as a basic framework.

All of the research suggested in this section could focus on the person's entire range and process of intentional change. Some researchers, however, will prefer a narrower focus.

Some might focus on one particular tool or resource, for example. How does the book by Browne (1973) or the O'Neills (1974) or Bolles (1980) or Tough (1980) fit into the person's process, and what difficulties and needs remain? How do libraries, medical doctors, courses, television, or some other particular resource fit into the process, and what else could such a resource contribute?

Other researchers might focus on one particular area of change. What are the difficulties and unmet needs in the human growth area, in spiritual growth, in understanding the world, in job change, in moving to another home, in becoming freer of sex-role stereotyping, in physical health, in child-raising and marriage enrichment, in basic education?

Still other researchers might focus on one particular aspect of the person's natural process of intentional change. They might intensively study one basic task or another, such as the detailed thought process in choosing the change or the difficulties in implementing it. They might study the sorts of changes that require no outside help, the sorts that require help from nonprofessionals or books, and the sorts that require various amounts of professional help.

A somewhat different line of research could focus on persons who are especially effective at choosing and managing their major changes. How do these highly successful changers go about the various tasks? How do they react to obstacles and doubts? In what ways does their process differ from the process followed by unsuccessful changers? What paths and methods and strategies do they choose? What are the secrets of their success? Principles and tips for all of us might emerge from such research.

# Chapter 8

# An Optimistic Future
# for Intentional Changes

Four main themes emerged from our 180 exploratory interviews and our 150 final interviews. As the interview results accumulated from various regions, I became more and more impressed by the consistency and importance of these four themes.

The first theme is the size and success of the intentional changes that men and women achieve. Only 4% failed to identify any intentional change at all from the previous two years. Of those who did identify a change, only 3% saw that change as small, trivial, petty, or unimportant. Over 30% of the changes were seen as huge, enormous, or of central importance. People changed their job or responsibilities, their self-perception and human relationships, their enjoyable activities and volunteer helping activities, their residence location and personal finances, and their physical health. The typical change was conspicuous enough to be noticed by seven people.

Most men and women are reasonably successful in achieving the changes that they choose. On the average, people achieve 80% of their target. Half of our interviewees had achieved 100%.

The high benefits from intentional changes provide the second salient theme in our interviews. Only 7% of the interviewees felt that their change had not contributed to their happiness, satisfaction with life, or well-being: 51% said their change had contributed

154

a large or enormous amount. In addition, most changes provided benefits to family, friends, employer, or other persons.

On the average, the changing person assumes about 70% of the responsibility for all of the subtasks involved in three major tasks: choosing the change, planning the strategy, and implementing the change. This central position and importance of the changing person is the third theme to emerge. Most changes are largely do-it-yourself right from the initial consideration of the potential change through to the implementation. Most people receive some help from at least one friend, family member, or other nonprofessional. Most of this help is obtained in one-to-one interaction rather than in a group. Much less help was received from counselors, educators, doctors, personnel managers, clergy, social workers, therapists, growth group leaders, and other people who help as part of their job. Professional help contributed a great deal to some change efforts, but was not even present in many successful efforts. Apparently people are quite capable of successfully choosing, planning, and achieving significant changes largely on their own, with some help from friends and other nonprofessionals.

At the same time we must note that people do encounter difficulties and obstacles. They sometimes have trouble clarifying and choosing the most appropriate target for change, discovering the best strategy for achieving that change, or actually implementing the chosen strategy. Despite their eventual success, people report that they could benefit from additional help and competence. This fourth theme leads us to consider fresh directions for practice and policy. How could we be more useful to people as they choose and guide their own changes?

## Significant Directions for Policy and Practice

In my optimistic vision of the future of intentional changes, I see policymakers and professional practitioners exploring several useful directions. The sum total of these fresh efforts will be highly significant for the entire range of intentional changes. Without unduly controlling or taking over the person's change efforts, we could be of great benefit to people in several new ways. As a result, people will be even more competent and successful than they are now in choosing and achieving important beneficial changes. Seven particular directions seem to me most likely to prove highly beneficial. I hope that many people in various occupations and settings will experiment with each direction.

1. Helping people become more competent at managing their intentional changes is a particularly fascinating, difficult, and important direction. We could try accomplishing this through print, tapes, television, groups, courses, counseling sessions, speeches, and workshops. Through these various means we could help people gain increased awareness and knowledge of intentional changes, simultaneously counteracting their self-deprecating and false beliefs about their own changes. Then people could more accurately see the effectiveness and success of their own natural change process. People could also become even more competent at performing the various tasks and steps required for successful changes, and at defining and obtaining the help they need.

2. Fresh sorts of help with goals and planning could be highly beneficial for many changes. Through a variety of media and settings and processes, we can develop better help with choosing goals and directions for change, and with choosing broad strategies and paths. Different people need help with different aspects, such as a broad framework or perspective for considering various particular options, an overview of the available changes and paths, an appropriate balance or budget for time and money, accurate self-insight and self-assessment, information about particular changes and methods, a series of intermediate goals, encouragement, and behavioral self-control principles.

3. We could improve and expand the information that is available about particular opportunities, methods, and resources. As information becomes more complete and accurate, and more readily available, people will choose and use more effective paths for their various changes.

4. Some people have been complaining recently about undue restrictions on their freedom to choose their resources for change. Each of us involved in any way in the professional helping enterprise should carefully study all sides of the issues and then thoughtfully work out a personal position that seems both fair and appropriate.

5. In addition to reducing any undue restrictions on freedom of choice, we can strive to widen even further the range of opportunities and resources available for change. Each agency, educational institution, professional practitioner, and field can usefully consider ways to provide additional content, methods, tools, paths, and media.

6. Improving the ongoing support available from nonprofessionals is another significant direction for fostering intentional changes. We could help a wide range of people become more effective as informal helpers. In addition, we could help people find individual nonprofessional helpers, a peer group, or a partner in change. Generally encouraging the self-help movement and the women's movement could also be useful.

7. Improving the effectiveness of professional and paraprofessional helpers is a particularly important direction for policy and practice. Helpers can improve by seeking feedback, discussing problems and new methods with colleagues, attending workshops and meetings, learning about intentional changes through reading or a few interviews. It is especially important for professional helpers to become adept at providing an optimum amount of control in the helping relationship, steering clear of the two extremes of overcontrol and undercontrol. Some efforts to shift from high professional control to shared responsibility for goals and strategy are already occurring in health care, counseling, personal growth groups, social work, adult learning, higher education, elementary and secondary education, and other fields. These efforts could be strengthened and expanded.

As policymakers, practitioners, student professionals-in-training, and their instructors explore these seven directions, they will enable people to choose even more appropriate changes than they do now, and to achieve them even more efficiently and successfully.

## Implications for Research

Several research directions, too, can contribute to improvement in intentional changes. As our understanding of these changes increases, our help and resources and other efforts will become more useful. Four research directions seem to me especially significant.

1. It would be useful and fascinating to study the place of intentional changes in all of the person's changes over the years. What percentage of all change is intentional? How beneficial and stressful are intentional changes compared to unintentional changes? In what ways do highly intentional changers differ from those whose changes are largely unintentional?

2. The data collected for this book give us a reasonably good picture of intentional changes. Now several additional surveys are

needed to study intentional changes in other countries or regions, in specific subcultures and occupational groups, and in particular areas of life. As the results of these further surveys become available, the picture will become more detailed and accurate.

3. During face-to-face interaction between a helper and another person, a variety of factors and forces, both inner and outer, sometimes contribute to helper overcontrol and to the person's passive submission. A few insightful, sensitive, thoughtful researchers could probably illuminate this complex and subtle interaction.

4. In the previous section, and in chapters 5 and 6, I have spelled out seven useful directions for facilitating intentional changes. Just how beneficial would each of these be for changers? Would some other direction be even more beneficial? What really are the unmet needs: from what additional help and competence would people especially benefit? As one step toward answering these questions, researchers might study the process that already occurs, including the tasks performed by the person and the help obtained with these tasks. They might also usefully study the person's difficulties, mistakes, doubts, inaccurate beliefs, and obstacles.

## Achieving the Full Potential

In North America and England, and presumably in other regions as well, most men and women choose and successfully achieve beneficial changes. They do this largely on their own, with some help from friends and family. If through some magic telescope one could observe this activity over the entire planet, one would be struck by how common and widespread it is, by the amount of time and personal energy devoted to it, and by its positive impact on human happiness and well-being.

Suppose a second magic telescope could be focused on the planet's total professional and institutional helping enterprise. We would see counselors, therapists, doctors, self-help books and magazines, classrooms, hospitals, workshops, conferences, professionally led groups, staff development departments, clinics, universities, schools, educational television and radio, cassettes, religious services, private lessons, social work agencies, agricultural and homemaking extension programs, correspondence courses, and so on.

Absorbed by observing these two huge and significant enterprises, we might begin to wonder how much they coincide. Are the two images coterminous? Are the two activities vitally linked? Do they nourish and encourage each other? Do they provide mutual aid?

I am struck by how separate and distant the two enterprises are at present. Even in intensive probing interviews, people report remarkably little help from professional helpers. People simply do not seek help from professionals with the bulk of their changes. At the same time, some professionals seem oblivious to, or ignorant of, the person's natural process of choosing and achieving a wide range of intentional changes. In their worst moments, a few professionals actually denigrate, discourage, undercut, or attack self-guided changes.

In the last few chapters I have been suggesting some relatively unexplored ways in which the professional and institutional helping enterprise could become more useful to the entire range of intentional human changes. I see enormous potential for each of these two activities to contribute much more to the other. As we continue to watch the two activities around the globe through our two magic telescopes, possibly we will see them become more closely linked and intertwined, providing mutual support and help to each other, synergistically achieving their full potential.

Not so many years ago, humankind found that it is not at the center of the physical universe, nor even of the solar system. The universe certainly does not revolve around us. We are not even at the center of our own galaxy, but are located somewhat insignificantly toward the edge of it.

For a moment, let us compare our galaxy with the entire range of intentional human changes: each of the billions of stars could represent one person's changes. The professional helping enterprise often assumes it is at the center of this galaxy: a few changes may occur without professional help, but they are peripheral and insignificant. A few professionals make an even more extreme assumption: they fail to realize that any intentional changes at all occur beyond those that are professionally guided.

As we explore the galaxy of intentional changes, we professionals discover that we are not as important and central as we thought we were. Not all intentional changes revolve around us; in fact, we are not even present in most changes. The central phenomenon in the galaxy of intentional changes turns out to be not professional help, but the person's own planning and process along with help from friends and family. Let's venture forth from our professional base and assumptions to explore the rest of the galaxy. Let's study the fascinating context within which our helping efforts occur. Let's immerse ourselves in the person's natural process of self-guided change and see how intentional changes actually occur in most people. Then we will be much better able to foster and facilitate this significant human activity.

By focusing on the entire range of major intentional changes, many institutions and professional fields may be united by this common focus. A fresh comprehensive or umbrella field may emerge.

A small pioneering group or network of like-minded persons in the 1980s might grow into a professional association in the 1990s. Such an association could spark workshops, conferences, and newsletters. Professional helpers might become committed to fostering the entire range of changes and feel a kinship with the total helping enterprise. Although loyal to their own particular professions (counseling, education, humanistic psychology, public health, and a dozen others), practitioners might also be interested in the interaction, cooperation, and kinship provided by an umbrella association for everyone involved in facilitating major intentional change in people aged 10 to 100.

Practitioners and researchers from various fields and movements can learn a great deal—about successful practices and past errors, for instance—from other fields. If the thousands and thousands of people employed in facilitating change were to join together, their power could be enormous. As I once said at a professional meeting, "Compared to the total population of the United States and the world, each movement is rather small. Useful interaction might produce far greater impact than continuing to be separated by a rarely crossed chasm" (Tough, 1972, p. 336).

A comprehensive field of research and theory-building, too, may eventually coalesce, focusing on the total range of intentional changes. A research journal, research and development centers, university courses, even an entire graduate department might be established.

More beneficial and efficient changes will result from these various innovations in practice, policy, and research. People will notice and treasure their own intentional changes, and will accurately see their thoughtfulness and success. They will choose changes that are highly beneficial to the well-being and happiness of themselves and others. They will be able to choose from a wide panorama of methods and resources for achieving their chosen changes, and will have ready access to full accurate information about these options. They will seek and receive highly effective professional help whenever needed, along with support and help from family and friends. They will cheerfully proceed to implement their changes with ease and grace. They will know deeply through experience that choosing and creating significant changes in oneself and one's life is a particularly fascinating and important human enterprise.

# Appendix

## The Interview Schedule

### Some Preliminary Notes for the Interviewer

In order to get an accurate deep understanding of intentional changes, it is essential that the interviews be sufficiently leisurely, with plenty of probing and dialogue.

Throughout the first part of the interview, you will probably have to dialogue at various times to help the person grasp the precise phenomenon and criteria. It may help if you use the phrase "intentional changes" or "intentional portion of the change." It may also help if the discussion shuttles back and forth between the actual change and the decision to change: talking about either one alone is misleading. Most important of all, you must keep clearly in mind the definition and criteria presented in chapter 1.

Throughout the interview, be sure both of you focus on the correct portion of the change. Exclude any portion of the actual change that was not chosen. Also, include only the *already-achieved* portion of the change. A *decision* to look for a better job can be included as a decision, but not as a completed change to a new job.

Dialogue may be particularly necessary to help the person capture the change (or the *intentional* portion of a change) for question 1. Changes are complex, many-faceted, and intertwined: as a result, there are often several ways of viewing and defining the focus of a change. Help the person work out the best one.

The change may become clearer if you ask this question regarding the change that is chosen: "Within this area, what exactly is *different* now—in you or your activities or your surroundings—compared to the time before your decision to change?"

Use a separate sheet for your notes until the answer to question 1 becomes fairly clear. Then record it on the data sheet.

These questions may be used freely for research or academic purposes, but may not be sold nor used for commercial purposes without written permission from the publisher. The author would appreciate information concerning any studies based on these interview questions.

## Interview Questions

During the past two years, you have probably experienced various changes in yourself, in your activities, and in your life.

Some of these changes probably happened accidentally, but today we'll focus on the *intentional* changes, the changes you *decided* to achieve.

Some of your changes were probably small or not very important. But today we will look at the changes that were especially large and important for you. In fact, our first step is to select your *largest, most important* change during the past two years. They don't have to be huge, earth-shattering changes! And I don't care how large or important it was to *other* people. All I need is the one change, out of all your intentional changes, that seems to *you* to be larger or more important than any other change you can recall.

Let me assure you that all the information you give me will be used only for research purposes, and I will certainly not attach your name to any of this information. You are free to ask any questions, of course, and to stop the interview at any time.

[Give sheet #1, which is reproduced here in figure 2. Point to appropriate parts of it during the rest of this paragraph.] Here's a summary chart. At some point you decided to change something about yourself or your life. Then you took one or more steps to achieve that change. And then you actually did achieve the change. Take your time looking over this sheet. Feel free to mark it if you wish.

[Point out the instructions at the top of the sheet. Dialogue about one or two tentative choices.]

Before you make the final selection of the largest change, I want you to recall *all* of your changes during the past two years that might qualify. But it's hard to remember all your changes, even the big important ones, over a two-year period. So I have a memory-jogging sheet here. It may help you recall some especially large change that you haven't mentioned yet.

Take your time. [Give sheet #2. After the person has gone through it reasonably carefully, move toward selecting the largest intentional change, which is question 1.]

1. What was the intentional change (or the intended *portion* of the change)? [Give concrete details if possible. Be sure that what you record is a *change,* and that it was *intentional.* Be sure that the change meets the criteria on sheet #1.]

2. What percentage of your desired change did you actually achieve? [Relate this question to the diagram if that will help the person understand.]

3–6. Here are four further questions. Just circle the answers that come closest to describing the intentional portion of your actual change. [Give sheet #3.]

7. Now let's turn our attention to three major tasks that you may have performed—or that someone else may have performed for you—in order to achieve your change. The top part of this sheet outlines the three tasks. [Give sheet #4. Then help the person understand the three tasks, and relate them to his or her particular change. Take plenty of time for this.]

The bottom part of the sheet lists various possibilities for who might have performed the task. For example, the first possibility on the list is you, and the second is books, booklets, etc. [Pause.]

Now let's look at the first major task, right at the top of the sheet. How would you divide the credit or responsibility for performing this task? That is, what percentage of the task was performed by you, and what percentage by each of the others in the list? I'm not just thinking of who actually made the final decision. No, what I'm thinking of is who or what played some part in the process of assessing the possible change, weighing its consequences, and so on. For instance, a *magazine* might have been very helpful by getting you to think about the change in the first place, or by getting you to see that such a change really would be possible for you. [Add possible examples for this person's particular change if you can.] Don't worry about being perfectly accurate with this question: just your best estimate. And don't bother including any category that was under 10%.

[Before you record the percentages, please be absolutely certain that they add up to 100. Also, in this question and the next two, whenever you get a percentage for b, c, d, or e, jot down a few words to identify the particular book, person, or group.]

8. Now let's do the same for the second task.

9 Now the third task: what were the percentages for that?

10. We've been talking about a change that was chosen and intentional. Can you think of any *un*intentional change over the past two years—in yourself or in your life—that is even larger and more significant than the change we've been discussing? [If the answer is YES, record the unintentional change or changes.]

11. Throughout the interview we have been talking about changes that you did achieve, at least partly. Looking back over the past two years, has there been some change that you certainly *wanted*, but did not achieve? [Record the desired change, and any hunches you have about the blocks or about what help/resources would have been useful.]

12. What is the highest educational qualification that you have completed?

13. Are you employed outside the home these days? What is your specific occupation?

14. Could you tell me your age? [If refused, give an estimate.]
[Interviewer records the following information after the interview.]

[15. Interviewer estimate of social class.]

[16. Male or female.]

[17. Member of which racial or ethnic group.]

From all of your intentional changes during the past two years, please select your largest, most important change. If in doubt between two changes, choose the one that will affect you and your life the most, or the one that will last longest.

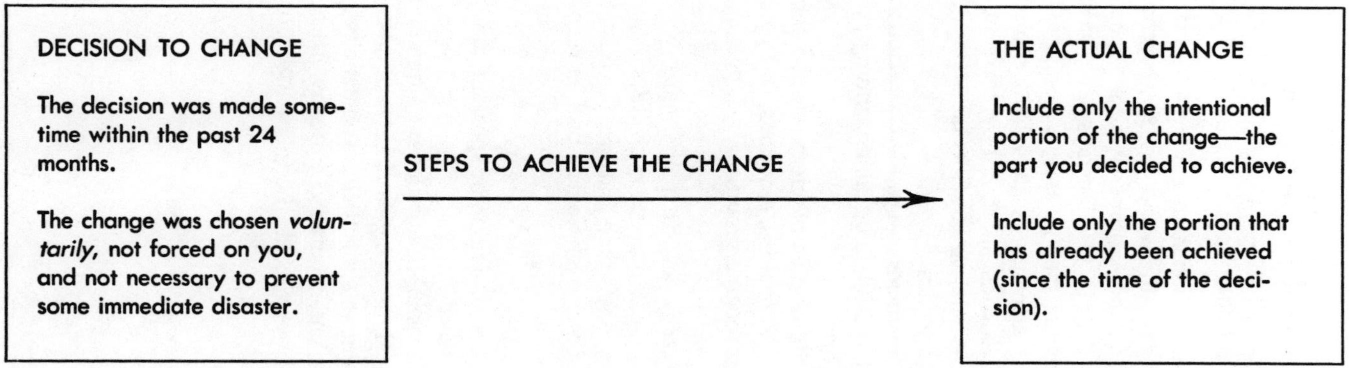

## DECISION TO CHANGE

The decision was made some-time within the past 24 months.

The change was chosen *voluntarily*, not forced on you, and not necessary to prevent some immediate disaster.

## STEPS TO ACHIEVE THE CHANGE

## THE ACTUAL CHANGE

Include only the intentional portion of the change—the part you decided to achieve.

Include only the portion that has already been achieved (since the time of the deci-sion).

**Figure 2.** Interview Handout Sheet # 1.

## SHEET #2

To help you recall your own major intentional changes over the past two years, here are some areas in which people sometimes change intentionally:

body; health; appearance; fitness; relaxation

knowledge of the world, history, psychology, etc.

personal finances; property; possessions

marriage; family relationships; child-raising; separation

home and car maintenance; decorating; furniture

enjoyable activities (social activities, travel, crafts, art, theater, music, friends, sport, hobby, recreation, vacation, etc.)

residence; living arrangements

goals and values

psychic awareness; expanded consciousness; ultimate reality

spiritual and religious understanding; relationship to God or to the world

voluntarily helping others; making a contribution

human relationships; emotions; self-perception; self-confidence

change through a group, course, person, book, kit, or TV program

lifestyle; activities; circle of friends

the meaning and purpose of life

managing one's time and life; the balance of various activities

reduce some psychological problem, emotional difficulty, or bad habit

reduce male-female stereotyping

reading speed; writing or speaking ability; problem-solving; or other basic skill

job; responsibilities; income; training; education

begin, end, or change a close relationship

assertiveness; authenticity; spontaneity

wisdom; understanding; empathy; caring

## SHEET #3

3. Which response comes closest to describing the size and importance of your change (or of the intended portion)?

   a. a huge or enormous change, or of central importance in my life
   b. a fairly large and important change
   c. a definite change with *some* relevance and importance in my life
   d. small, trivial, petty, unimportant

4. How much has this change contributed to your happiness, your satisfaction with life, or your well-being?

   a. an enormous amount
   b. a large amount
   c. some definite benefit
   d. little or nothing
   e. it has done me more harm than good

5. Now let's imagine a certain situation for a moment. Let's imagine that you describe your change to all your friends, relatives, neighbors, people at work, and everyone else who knows you. And then you say to each of these people, "Have you noticed this change (or already heard about it)?" Approximately how many would say yes? (Circle your best guess.)

   zero  1  2  3  4  5  6  7  8  9  10 over 10

6. Let's set aside your own benefits for a moment, and look at any benefits for *other* people. Your change might already have been of some benefit to your family, your friends and relatives, your boss, other people in your organization, colleagues in your field, and so on. To what extent has your change provided some benefit to people other than yourself?

   a. only to a small extent
   b. medium amount; of some definite benefit to at least one or two persons
   c. to a fairly large extent

## SHEET #4

### Three Tasks

1. Deciding to go ahead with this particular change. As part of making this decision, you or someone else or a book might have examined various aspects of your life, obtained information, identified a tentative possible change, estimated the costs and benefits of this change, and so on.

2. Planning the strategy and deciding the steps for achieving the change.

3. Actually taking the steps for achieving the change.

### Who Performed the Task?

a. You.

b. Books, booklets, magazines, television, films, tapes, phonograph records.

c. A person who was paid to help, or was doing so as part of his or her job, or was designated by some organization to help, or was trained to help—and your interaction with this person was individual one-to-one interaction (possibly with one or two other persons also present).

d. A group in which the same sort of person as above (paid, employed, designated, or trained to help) was the leader or at least was an important resource. (The group, class, workshop, or audience could be of any size, as long as it had at least four persons meeting in the same room.)

e. A group of people who met fairly regularly, and who almost always met *without* a professional or expert as the leader or resource person.

f. One or more family members, friends, relatives, acquaintances, coworkers, or neighbors—in individual one-to-one interaction (possibly with one or two other persons also present).

# Data Sheet

1.



2.       3.       4.       5.       6.


[Please be sure that each of the next three lines adds up to 100%.]

7. a      b      c      d      e      f

8. a      b      c      d      e      f

9. a      b      c      d      e      f

10. NO      YES:


11.


12.


13.


14.       15.


16. F      M


17.

### Supplementary Questions for Studying Difficulties, Task Details, and Additional Needs

[Question 6A is best inserted after question 6, and questions 9A through 9G are best inserted after question 9.]

6A. Looking back over your total experience in choosing, planning, and achieving this change, what was the one most *difficult* part of the whole thing for you?

9A. Now, going back to the first task, I'm interested in knowing some of the things you *did* during that task—what you took into consideration, any information you gathered, how you arrived at the decision to go ahead with this change, and any other step you took.

9B. Moving on to the second task, just what did you do during that task? For instance, did you gather any information, make a list of different possibilities, or take any other steps in order to plan your strategy?

9C. The third task refers to actually taking the steps for achieving the change. What were your major steps or methods for achieving your change?

9D. This next question applies to all three major tasks that we've been discussing—the three tasks at the top of your sheet. Suppose with each of your tasks and decisions, additional help had been available in the form of a book, some other form of printed material, a tape, a film, or a TV program. Is there anything you would have liked additional help with? [If necessary, probe with the following question: What sorts of additional help would you have liked?]

9E. Suppose additional help for all three tasks had been available in the form of a particularly helpful or encouraging *person,* an expert, a group, or a professional. In what ways could such a person or group have been useful for you?

9F. Now let's imagine some magic; let's imagine someone had waved a magic wand two years ago, and as a result you had an incredibly high level of skill, competence, expertise, and confidence in performing the various aspects of all three tasks. Was there any sort of skill or expertise—in addition to what you already had—that would have been especially beneficial for you in moving ahead with your change?

9G. Why did you want this change? In this question I'm looking far ahead to the ultimate benefits you expected—the benefits that you anticipated eventually from this change.

# References

Adams, J., Hayes, J., and Hopson, B. *Transition: Understanding and Managing Personal Change.* London: Martin Robertson, 1976.

Allender, J.S., and Silberman, M.L. "Three Varieties of Student-Directed Learning: A Research Report." *Journal of Humanistic Psychology,* 1979, 19 (1), 79–83.

American Psychological Association. "Guidelines for Psychologists Conducting Growth Groups." *American Psychologist,* 1973, 28, 933.

Antonucci, T., Kulka, R.A., and Douvan, E.M. "Informal Social Supports in 1957 and 1976." In M.B. Smith (Chair), "Americans View Their Mental Health: 1957–1976." Symposium presented at the annual meeting of the American Psychological Association, Toronto, September 1978.

Armstrong, D. "Adult Learners of Low Educational Attainment: The Self-Concepts, Backgrounds, and Educative Behavior of Average and High Learning Adults of Low Educational Attainment." Doctoral dissertation, University of Toronto, 1971. *Dissertation Abstracts International,* 1972, 33, 944A–945A. (Available from National Library of Canada: Canadian Theses on Microfilm no. 11532.)

173

Armstrong, J.S. "The Use of Time Contracts in Formal Education." Paper presented at the conference of the Association for Business Simulation and Experiential Learning, Dallas, April 1980.

Bates, H.M. "A Phenomenological Study of Adult Learners: Participants' Experiences of a Learner-Centered Approach." Unpublished doctoral dissertation, Ontario Institute for Studies in Education, University of Toronto, 1979.

Bell, R., and Coplans, J. *Decisions Decisions: Game Theory and You.* New York: Norton, 1976.

Berte, N.R. (Ed.). *Individualizing Education through Contract Learning.* University: University of Alabama Press, 1975.

Blackwell, D. "Major Intentional Changes among Adult Males in King Township." Unpublished doctoral dissertation, Ontario Institute for Studies in Education, University of Toronto, 1981.

Bolles, R.N. *What Color Is Your Parachute? A Practical Manual for Job-Hunters & Career Changers.* Berkeley: Ten Speed Press, 1980.

Boulding, E. *The Underside of History: A View of Women through Time.* Boulder: Westview, 1976.

Boulding, E. *Children's Rights and the Wheel of Life.* New Brunswick, N.J.: Transaction, 1979a.

Boulding, E. "The Learning Stance and the Experience Worlds of Women." In G.M. Healy and W.L. Ziegler (Eds.), *The Learning Stance: Essays in Celebration of Human Learning.* Final Report of the Learning Stance Project sponsored by the Syracuse Research Corporation under contract with the National Institute of Education. Unpublished manuscript, 1979b, pp. 1–39.

Bradley, A.P., Jr. *The Empire State College Mentor: An Emerging Role.* Saratoga Springs, N.Y.: Office of Evaluation and Research, Empire State College, 1975.

Bramucci, R.J. "A Factoral Examination of the Self-Empowerment Construct." Doctoral dissertation, University of Oregon, 1977. *Dissertation Abstracts International,* 1978, 38, 5087B. (University Microfilms no. 78-2507.)

Brand, S. *The Next Whole Earth Catalog: Access to Tools.* New York: Random House, 1980.

Browne, H. *How I Found Freedom in an Unfree World.* New York: Macmillan, 1973.

Calvert, R., Jr., and Draves, W.A. *Free Universities and Learning Referral Centers, 1978.* Washington, D.C.: National Center for Education Statistics, 1978.

Caplan, G., and Killilea, M. (Eds.). *Support Systems and Mutual Help.* New York: Grune & Stratton, 1976.

Carr, D.W. "The Agent and the Learner: A Study of Critical Incidents and Contexts in Assisted Library Learning." Unpublished doctoral dissertation, Rutgers University, 1979.

Castaneda, C. *Journey to Ixtlan: The Lessons of Don Juan.* New York: Simon & Schuster, 1972.

Chamberlin, J. *On Our Own: Patient-Controlled Alternatives to the Mental Health System.* New York: Hawthorn, 1978.

Cheren, M. "Facilitating the Transition from External Direction in Learning to Greater Self-Direction in Learning in Educational Institutions: A Case Study in Individualized Open System Post-Secondary Education." Doctoral dissertation, University of Massachusetts, 1978a. *Dissertation Abstracts International,* 1978a, 39 (3), 1362A. (University Microfilms no. 78–16246.)

Cheren, M. *A Manual for Program Advisors, 1978/79.* Washington, D.C.: Campus-Free College, 1978b.

Coates, T.J., and Thoresen, C.E. *How to Sleep Better: A Drug-Free Program for Overcoming Insomnia.* Englewood Cliffs, N.J.: Prentice-Hall, 1977.

Coates, T.J., and Thoresen, C.E. "Behavioral Self-Control and Educational Practice or Do We Really Need Self-Control?" In D.C. Berliner (Ed.), *Review of Research in Education, 7.* Washington, D.C.: American Educational Research Association, 1979.

Collins, A.H., and Pancoast, D.L. *Natural Helping Networks: A Strategy for Prevention.* Washington, D.C.: National Association of Social Workers, 1974.

Combs, A.W. *Florida Studies in the Helping Professions.* Gainesville: University of Florida Press, 1969.

Combs, A.W., Avila, D.L., and Purkey, W.W. *Helping Relationships: Basic Concepts for the Helping Professions.* (2nd ed.) Boston: Allyn & Bacon, 1978.

Cooper, S., and others. *Self-Directed Continuing Education in*

*Nursing.* Kansas City, Mo.: American Nurses' Association, 1978.

Coyne, J., and Hebert, T. *This Way Out: A Guide to Alternatives to Traditional College Education in the United States, Europe and the Third World.* New York: Dutton, 1972.

Cross, K.P. *The Missing Link: Connecting Adult Learners to Learning Resources.* New York: College Entrance Examination Board, 1978.

Crystal, J.C., and Bolles, R.N. *Where Do I Go from Here with My Life?* New York: Seabury, 1974.

Daloz, L.A. "Now They're Competent . . . So What?" *Educational Technology,* 1978, 18 (10), 22–26.

DeCharms, R. *Enhancing Motivation: Change in the Classroom.* New York: Irvington, 1976.

Della-Dora, D., and Blanchard, L.J. (Eds.). *Moving toward Self-Directed Learning: Highlights of Relevant Research and of Promising Practices.* Alexandria, Va.: Association for Supervision and Curriculum Development, 1979.

DeMause, L. (Ed.). *The History of Childhood.* New York: Psychohistory Press, 1974.

Ellis, A. "Rational-Emotive Therapy and Self-Help Theory." In G.M. Rosen (Chair), "Nonprescription Psychotherapies: Symposium on Do-It-Yourself Treatments." Symposium presented at the annual meeting of the American Psychological Association, San Francisco, August 1977. (Available as ERIC Document no. ED 147 735).

Faraday, A. *The Dream Game.* New York: Harper & Row, 1976.

Farber, J. *The Student as Nigger: Essays and Stories.* New York: Pocket Books, 1970.

Farquharson, W.A.F. "Peers as Helpers: Personal Change in Members of Self-Help Groups in Metropolitan Toronto." Doctoral dissertation, University of Toronto, 1975. *Dissertation Abstracts International,* 1978, 38 (10), 5848A. (Available from National Library of Canada: Canadian Theses on Microfiche no. 27841.)

Farson, R. *Birthrights.* New York: Macmillan, 1974.

Farson, R. "The Technology of Humanism." *Journal of Humanistic Psychology,* 1978, 18 (2), 5–35.

Filson, G.C. "Major Personal Changes in a Group of Canadians Working in Nigeria." Doctoral dissertation, University of Toronto, 1975. *Dissertation Abstracts International,* 1977, 38 (6), 3210A–3211A. (Available from National Library of Canada: Canadian Theses on Microfiche no. 31212.)

Fischer, C.T., and Brodsky, S.L. (Eds.). *Client Participation in Human Services: The Prometheus Principle.* New Brunswick, N.J.: Transaction, 1978.

Ford, G.A., and Lippitt, G.L. *Planning Your Future: A Workbook for Personal Goal Setting.* San Diego, Calif.: University Associates, 1976.

Freire, P. *Pedagogy of the Oppressed.* New York: Herder and Herder, 1970.

Friedman, M. *Capitalism and Freedom.* Chicago: University of Chicago Press, 1962.

Friedman, M., and Friedman, R. *Free to Choose: A Personal Statement.* New York: Harcourt Brace Jovanovich, 1980.

Friedman, T.B. "Self-Testing, Continued Competence, and Relicensure." Paper presented at the annual meeting of the American Psychological Association, Toronto, August 1978. (Available as ERIC Document no. ED 172 079).

Gartner, A., and Riessman, F. *Self-Help in the Human Services.* San Francisco: Jossey-Bass, 1977.

Gibb, J.R. *Trust: A New View of Personal and Organizational Development.* Los Angeles: Guild of Tutors Press, International College, 1978.

Gibbons, M., and Phillips, G. "Helping Students through the Self-Education Crisis." *Phi Delta Kappan,* 1978, 60 (4), 296–300.

Gordon, T. *P.E.T.: Parent Effectiveness Training.* New York: Wyden, 1970.

Governing Council of the New World Alliance. *A Transformation Platform: The Dialogue Begins.* Washington, D.C.: New World Alliance, 1981.

Grey, M.G., and Shirreff, E. *Thoughts on Self-Culture, Addressed to Women.* Boston: Crosby & Nichols, 1851.

Griffin, V. "Self-Directed Adult Learners and Learning." *Learning* (Canadian Association for Adult Education), 1978, 2 (1), 6–8, and 1979, 2 (2), 12–15.

Grinspoon, L., and Bakalar, J.B. *Psychedelic Drugs Reconsidered.* New York: Basic Books, 1979.

Grof, S. *Realms of the Human Unconscious: Observations from LSD Research.* New York: Viking, 1975.

Gross, R. *The Lifelong Learner.* New York: Simon & Schuster, 1977.

Gross, S.J. "Consumer Self-Protection as an Alternative to Licensing." *Association for Humanistic Psychology Newsletter,* June 1978a, p. 8.

Gross, S.J. "The Myth of Professional Licensing." *American Psychologist,* 1978b, 33 (11), 1009–1016.

Gurin, G., Veroff, J., and Feld, S. *Americans View Their Mental Health.* New York: Basic Books, 1960.


Harris, M. "Teaching Children at Home: The Legal and Emotional Challenges." *New Age,* 1979, 5 (3), 41–46.

Harrison, R. "Self-Directed Learning: A Radical Approach to Educational Design." *Simulation & Games,* 1977, 8 (1), 73–94.

Heffernan, J.M., Macy, F.U., and Vickers, D.F. *Educational Brokering: A New Service for Adult Learners.* Syracuse: National Center for Educational Brokering, 1976.

Heron, J. *Catharsis in Human Development.* London: British Postgraduate Medical Federation, University of London, 1977.

Holmes, T.H., and Rahe, R.H. "The Social Readjustment Rating Scale." *Journal of Psychosomatic Research,* 1967, 11, 213–218.

Home, A.M. "Change in Women's Consciousness-Raising Groups: A Study of Four Types of Change and of Some Factors Associated with Them." Doctoral dissertation, University of Toronto, 1978. (Available from National Library of Canada: Canadian Theses on Microfiche no. 38744.)

Houle, C.O. *The Inquiring Mind.* Madison: University of Wisconsin Press, 1961.

Houle, C.O. *The External Degree.* San Francisco: Jossey-Bass, 1973.

Howell, M.C. *Helping Ourselves: Families and the Human Network.* Boston: Beacon, 1975.


Illich, I. *Tools for Conviviality.* New York: Harper & Row, 1973.

Illich, I. *Toward a History of Needs.* New York: Pantheon, 1978.

Jones, R. *The Acorn People.* New York: Bantam, 1977.

Josephs, M.J. "A Competency-Based Program." In R.K. Loring, C. LeGates, M.J. Josephs, and J. O'Neill, *Adapting Institutions to the Adult Learner: Experiments in Progress.* 1978 National Conference Series. Washington, D.C.: American Association for Higher Education, 1978, pp. 12–16.

Kazdin, A.E. *History of Behavioral Modification: Experimental Foundations of Contemporary Research.* Baltimore: University Park Press, 1978.

Keeney, W. (Ed.). *Self-Directed Professional Development.* Newton, Kansas: Growth Associates, Prairie View Inc., 1980.

Kirschenbaum, H. *On Becoming Carl Rogers.* New York: Delacorte, 1979.

Klein, F. *The Bisexual Option: A Concept of One Hundred Percent Intimacy.* New York: Arbor House, 1978.

Knowles, M.S. *Self-Directed Learning: A Guide for Learners and Teachers.* Chicago: Follett, 1975.

Kulka, R.A. "Seeking Formal Help for Personal Problems: 1957–1976." In M.B. Smith (Chair), "Americans View Their Mental Health: 1957–1976." Symposium presented at the annual meeting of the American Psychological Association, Toronto, September 1978.

Lakein, A. *How to Get Control of Your Time and Your Life.* New York: Wyden, 1973.

Lande, N. *Mindstyles Lifestyles: A Comprehensive Overview of Today's Life-Changing Philosophies.* Los Angeles: Price/Stern/Sloan, 1976.

Lewis, G.R. "A Comparative Study of Learning Networks in the United States." Unpublished doctoral dissertation, Northwestern University, 1978.

Lewis, G.R., and Kinishi, D.R. *The Learning Exchange: What It Is, How It Works, How You Can Set Up a Similar Program for Your Community.* Evanston, Ill.: The Learning Exchange, 1977.

Lieberman, M.A., and others. *Self-Help Groups for Coping with Crisis: Origins, Members, Processes, and Impact.* San Francisco: Jossey-Bass, 1979.

Lifelong Learning Project. *Lifelong Learning and Public Policy.* Washington, D.C.: U.S. Government Printing Office, 1978.

Lisman, D., and Ohliger, J. "Must We All Go Back to School?" *The Progressive*, 1978, 42 (10), 35–37.

Loevinger, J., Wessler, R., and Redmore, C. *Measuring Ego Development*. Vol. 1: *Construction and Use of a Sentence Completion Test*. San Francisco: Jossey-Bass, 1970.

Loughary, J.W., and Ripley, T.M. *Career and Life Planning Guide*. Chicago: Follett, 1976.

Luikart, C. "Social Networks and Self-Planned Adult Learning." *University of North Carolina Extension Bulletin*, 1977, 61 (2), entire issue.

Lyon, H.C., Jr. "Humanistic Education for Lifelong Learning." *International Review of Education*, 1974, 10 (4), 502–505.

McCatty, C.A.M. "Patterns of Learning Projects Among Professional Men." Doctoral dissertation, University of Toronto, 1973. *Dissertation Abstracts International*, 1974, 35, 323A–324A. (Available from National Library of Canada: Canadian Theses on Microfilm no. 16647.)

McGinnis, P.S. "Major Personal Changes in Forty Returned CUSO Volunteers." Doctoral dissertation, University of Toronto, 1975. *Dissertation Abstracts International*, 1977, 38 (6), 3215A–3216A. (Available from National Library of Canada: Canadian Theses on Microfiche no. 33094.)

MacKenzie, N., Postgate, R., and Scupham, J. *Open Learning: Systems and Problems in Post-Secondary Education*. Paris: Unesco Press, 1975.

McKnight, J. "Professionalized Service and Disabling Help." In I. Illich and others, *Disabling Professions*. London: Marion Boyars, 1977, pp. 69–91.

Maslow. A.H. "Toward a Humanistic Biology." *American Psychologist*, 1969, 24 (8), 724–735.

Masters, R., and Houston, J. *Mind Games*. New York: Viking, 1972.

Matson, K. *The Psychology Today Omnibook of Personal Development*. New York: Morrow, 1977.

Miller, G.A. "Psychology as a Means of Promoting Human Welfare." *American Psychologist*, 1969, 24, 1063–1075.

Miller, G.P. *Life Choices: How to Make the Critical Decisions— About Your Education, Career, Marriage, Family, Life Style*. New York: Crowell, 1978.

Miller, S., Nunnally, E.W., and Wackman, D.B. *Alive and Aware: How to Improve Your Relationships through Better Communications.* Minneapolis, Minn.: Interpersonal Communication Programs, Inc., 1975.

Miller, W.R. "Effectiveness of Nonprescription Therapies for Problem Drinkers." Unpublished manuscript, 1978. (Available as ERIC Document no. ED 166 612.)

Mortimer, J.T., and Simmons, R.G. "Adult Socialization." *Annual Review of Sociology,* 1978, 4, 421–454.

Moustakas, C.E. *Turning Points.* Englewood Cliffs, N.J.: Prentice-Hall, 1977.

Nacke, M. "Life After the Workshop: Effects of the Survey of Resources for Development in Ministry Workshop." Unpublished doctoral dissertation, University of Toronto, 1979.

Naranjo, C. *The One Quest.* New York: Viking, 1972.

Neehall, J. "Intentional and Unintentional Change Among a Group of Canadian Adults." First draft of doctoral dissertation, University of Toronto (Ontario Institute for Studies in Education), 1981.

Newsom, R. "Lifelong Learning in London: 1558–1640." *Lifelong Learning: The Adult Years,* 1977, 1 (4), pp. 4, 5, 19–21.

O'Neill, N., and O'Neill, G. *Shifting Gears: Finding Security in a Changing World.* New York: Evans, 1974.

Ontario Society for Training and Development. *Competency Analysis for Trainers: A Personal Planning Guide.* Toronto: Ontario Society for Training and Development, 1979.

Pancoast, D.L. "A Method of Assisting Natural Helping Networks." In R.D. Young (Chair), "Social Support Networks and Socially Indigenous Helpers." Symposium presented at the annual meeting of the American Psychological Association, Toronto, September 1978. (Available as ERIC Document no. ED 170 648.)

Patterson, S.L. "Natural Helping Approaches: Implications for Humanizing Professional Practice." In R.D. Young (Chair), "Social Support Networks and Socially Indigenous Helpers." Symposium presented at the annual meeting of the American Psychological Association, Toronto, September 1978.

Penland, P.R. *Self-Planned Learning in America.* Pittsburgh: University of Pittsburgh Bookstore, 1977.

Posluns, E. "The Change Process of Women Becoming Liberated from Sex-Role Stereotypes." Unpublished doctoral dissertation, Ontario Institute for Studies in Education, University of Toronto, 1981.

Rodin, J. In J. Rodin (Chair), "Power, Freedom, Choice, Contingency: Control by Any Other Name. . . ." Discussion presented at the annual meeting of the American Psychological Association, Toronto, August 1978.

Rogers, C.R. *Carl Rogers on Personal Power.* New York: Delacorte, 1977.

Rogers, E.M., and Shoemaker, F.F. *Communication of Innovation.* (2nd ed.) New York: Free Press, 1971.

Rosen, B. "Written Treatment Contracts: Their Use in Planning Treatment Programs for In-Patients." *British Journal of Psychiatry,* 1978, 133, 410–415.

Roszak, T. "The Manifesto of the Person (From the Plenary Talk to the World Symposium on Humanity, Vancouver, 1977)." *New Directions,* 1977, No. 29–30, pp. 22–33.

Roth, J.A. "Staff and Client Control Strategies in Urban Hospital Emergency Services." *Urban Life and Culture,* 1972, 1 (April), 39–60.

Rothbard, M.N. *For a New Liberty: The Libertarian Manifesto.* (Rev. ed.) New York: Macmillan, 1978.

Samuels, M., and Bennett, H. *The Well Body Book.* New York: Random House/Bookworks, 1973.

Sarason, S.B., and others. *Human Services and Resources Networks: Rationale, Possibilities, and Public Policy.* San Francisco: Jossey-Bass, 1977.

Scholz, N.T., and others. *How to Decide: A Guide for Women.* New York: College Entrance Examination Board, 1975.

Schrag, P. *Mind Control.* New York: Pantheon, 1978.

Schutz, W. *Profound Simplicity.* London: Turnstone, 1979.

Scott, D. "Developing Learning Projects to Improve Interpersonal Skills: A Workshop and Helping Resources for Educational Administrators." Unpublished doctoral dissertation, Ontario Institute for Studies in Education, University of Toronto, 1981.

Sehnert, K.W. *How to Be Your Own Doctor—Sometimes.* New York: Grosset & Dunlap, 1975.

Shapiro, B.Z. *Symposium Papers: Helping Networks and the Welfare State, University of Toronto, May 13-15, 1980.* Toronto: Faculty of Social Work, University of Toronto, 1980.

Simon, S.B. *Meeting Yourself Halfway: Thirty-One Values Clarification Strategies for Daily Living.* Niles, Ill.: Argus Communications, 1974.

Smith, R.M. *Learning How to Learn in Adult Education.* Information Series No. 10. DeKalb: ERIC Clearinghouse in Career Education, Northern Illinois University, 1976. (Also available as ERIC Document no. ED 132 245.)

Smith, R.M. *Learning How to Learn: Applied Theory for Adults.* Chicago: Follett, 1982.

Society for the Advancement of Continuing Education for Ministry. *Planned Continuing Education: A Study of Needs Assessment Processes.* Collegeville, Pa.: Society for the Advancement of Continuing Education for Ministry, 1978.

Spragg, S.E. "Taking Charge: The Self-Directed Life." *Denver Open Network News,* 1978, 1 (3), 3.

Stanchina, C.H. *Two Years of Autonomy: Practise and Outlook.* Nancy, France: Nancy Univ., 1976. (Available as ERIC Document no. ED 148 127.)

Stevens, J.O. *Awareness: Exploring, Experimenting, Experiencing.* Walnut Creek, Calif.: Real People Press, 1971.

Strong, M. "The Autonomous Adult Learner: The Idea of Autonomous Learning, the Capabilities and Perceived Needs of the Autonomous Learner." Unpublished master's thesis, University of Nottingham, 1977.

Strupp, H.H., and others. *Psychotherapy for Better or Worse.* New York: Aronson, 1977.

Sundberg, N.D., Snowden, L.R., and Reynolds, W.M. "Toward Assessment of Personal Competence and Incompetence in Life Situations." *Annual Review of Psychology,* 1978, 29, 179-221.

Task Panel on Community Support Systems. "Report." In *Report of the President's Commission on Mental Health.* Vol. 2: *Task Panel Reports.* Washington, D.C.: Government Printing Office, 1978, pp. 139-235.

Taylor, I. *Self-Cultivation Recommended, or Hints to a Youth Leaving School.* Boston: Wells & Lilly, 1820.

Taylor, P. "Inside." *New Age,* 1978, 4 (6), 4.

Thomas, L.E. "Mid-Career Changes: Self-Selected or Externally Mandated?" *Vocational Guidance Quarterly,* 1977, 25 (4), 320–328.

Thomas, L.F., and Harri-Augstein, E.S. *The Self-Organised Learner and the Printed Word.* Uxbridge, England: Centre for the Study of Human Learning, Brunel University, 1977. (Also available as ERIC Document no. ED 159 594.)

Thomas, P.F. "The Influence of Dreams in the Personal Changes of Forty Adults." Unpublished doctoral dissertation, University of Toronto, 1978.

Toffler, A. *The Third Wave.* New York: Morrow, 1980.

Tough, A. *Learning Without a Teacher: A Study of Tasks and Assistance during Adult Self-Teaching Projects.* Toronto: Ontario Institute for Studies in Education, 1967. Reissued in 1981 with an updated bibliography of recent research.

Tough, A. *Why Adults Learn: A Study of the Major Reasons for Beginning and Continuing a Learning Project.* Toronto: Ontario Institute for Studies in Education, 1968. (Also available as ERIC Document no. ED 025 688.)

Tough, A. "Two Movements Interacting: Human Potential and Adult Education." *Adult Leadership,* 1972, 20, 335–336.

Tough, A. *The Adult's Learning Projects: A Fresh Approach to Theory and Practice in Adult Learning.* (2nd ed.) San Diego: University Associates (Learning Concepts), and Toronto: Ontario Institute for Studies in Education, 1979.

Tough, A. *Expand Your Life.* New York: College Board, 1980.

Unesco. *Thinking Ahead: Unesco and the Challenges of Today and Tomorrow.* Paris: Unesco, 1977.

Vasconcellos, J. "Humanizing Politics." *New Age,* 1978, 4 (5), 32–38.

Vasconcellos, J. *A Liberating Vision: Politics for Growing Humans.* San Luis Obispo, Calif.: Impact, 1979.

Veroff, J. "Measures of General Well-Being over a Generation." In M.B. Smith (Chair), "Americans View Their Mental Health: 1957–1976." Symposium presented at the annual meeting of the American Psychological Association, Toronto, September 1978.

Wallen, N.E., and Travers, R.M.W. "Analysis and Investigation of Teaching Methods." In N.L. Gage (Ed.), *Handbook of Research on Teaching.* Chicago: Rand McNally, 1963, pp. 448–505.

Wickett, R.E.Y. "Adult Learning Projects Related to Spiritual Growth." Doctoral dissertation, University of Toronto, 1977. *Dissertation Abstracts International,* 1977, 39 (7), 3987A–3988A. (Available from National Library of Canada: Canadian Theses on Microfiche no. 36868.)

Williamson, J.D., and Danaher, K. *Self-Care in Health.* London: Croom Helm, 1978.

Worthington, H., and Scanlon, K. "Board Demands Birth Report." *Toronto Star,* December 1, 1979, p. A3.

Youngblood, G. "The Mass Media and the Future of Desire." *CoEvolution Quarterly,* 1977. No. 16 (Winter 1977/78), pp. 6–17.

Ziegler, W.L. *The Future of Adult Education and Learning in the United States.* Final Report Prepared for Division of Adult Education, U.S. Office of Education, under Project Grant OEG-0-73-5232. Syracuse: Educational Policy Research Center, Syracuse Research Corporation, 1977a.

Ziegler, W.L. *An Instrument for the Analysis of Policies for and Programs in Lifelong Learning.* Syracuse: Syracuse Research Corporation, 1977b.

# Acknowledgments

Albert Ellis, ERIC Microfiche ED 147 735. APA Symposium on Nonprescription Psychotherapies. Copyright © by the Institute for Rational-Emotive Therapy.

Robert McIntyre, excerpt from "Stopping." Reprinted by permission.

Diane L. Pancoast, ERIC Document ED 170 648.

Carl Rogers, *Carl Rogers on Personal Power,* Delacorte Press. Copyright © 1977 by Carl Rogers.

Keith W. Sehnert, M.D., and Howard Eisenberg, *How to Be Your Own Doctor—Sometimes.* Copyright © 1975, 1981 by Keith W. Sehnert, M.D., and Howard Eisenberg. Reprinted by permission of Grosset & Dunlap, Inc.

Susan Ellis Spragg, "Taking Charge: The Self-Directed Life," *Open Network News,* September 1978, p. 3.

Peggy Taylor, *New Age* Magazine, November 1978. Reprinted by permission. Copyright © 1978 by New Age Communications, Inc. (Box 1200, Allston, MA 02134; subscriptions $15/yr.) All rights reserved.

# Index

# About the Author

Allen Tough is a professor at the Ontario Institute for Studies in Education and at the University of Toronto. He received the B.A. degree in psychology (1958) and the M.A. degree in education and psychology (1962) from the University of Toronto. During his research for the Ph.D. degree, awarded by the University of Chicago in 1965, he focused on the psychology of intentional adult learning. That research marked the beginning of his long-term interest in the person's major efforts to learn and change, both professionally guided and self-guided.

Tough (rhymes with stuff) is the author of four previous books: *Learning Without a Teacher* (1967), *Why Adults Learn* (1968), *The Adult's Learning Projects* (2nd ed., 1979), and *Expand Your Life* (1980). In addition, he has contributed twenty papers and chapters to the professional literature and has made a hundred presentations at conferences and seminars. His speaking and research have taken him to many parts of the United States and Canada, and to Australia, France, Ghana, India, New Zealand, and the United Kingdom. He has presented papers at national and international meetings in the fields of adult and continuing education, higher education, psychology, humanistic psychology, and futures studies. His research has been cited widely and has sparked nearly fifty further studies in seven countries.

Beginning his professional career in 1959 as an English teacher and guidance counselor in a suburban high school, Tough has been teaching graduate-level courses in such subjects as psychology, sociology, adult education, and futures studies since 1964. He has served as consulting editor of *Adult Education,* as chairperson of the National Seminar on Adult Education Research, as first vice-chairperson of the 1979 Unesco meeting of European experts on autonomous learning, and as consultant on adult learning to several universities and research projects.